SO
NOW
WHAT?

SO
NOW
WHAT?

HARNESSING GRIEF AFTER
LIFE'S MAJOR LOSSES

ALEXANDRA MCGROARTY

atmosphere press

For MJM – forever my always

TABLE OF CONTENTS

CHAPTER ONE – UNDEFINING GRIEF   3

What you already know   3

Stages of grief   7

Beyond the Five Stages   10

CHAPTER TWO – THE DEATH-DENYING CULTURE   14

Habits of death denial   15

Why is death-denial a problem?   17

Other viewpoints from the world   18

Moving toward death acceptance   23

CHAPTER THREE – BEING THERE   26

What to say when someone dies   26

What not to say when someone is grieving – and why   30

Supporting someone experiencing grief   32

The grace period   34

CHAPTER FOUR – GUILT, BLAME, AND ANGER   36

But first...shock, denial, and unreality   36

Guilt   38

Blame   39

What use is guilt or blame?   41

"But you have nothing to feel guilty about."   42

Anger   43

Coping with guilt   44

Learning from guilt   46

CHAPTER FIVE - WHEN YOU NEED HELP 47

When to reach out 48

What help is available? 50

Conclusion 53

CHAPTER SIX - CONSULTING A MEDIUM 54

How it started 55

Describing a session 56

Questions you may have 58

Conclusion 61

CHAPTER SEVEN - THE GRIEVING PARENT 62

How children of different ages perceive death 62

What can parents do for grieving children? 65

Taking care of yourself 69

When to seek professional grief counseling
for children 72

Healing together 73

CHAPTER EIGHT - RITUALS THAT HONOR AND REMEMBER 74

Ideas for inspiration 74

When you can stop a ritual 82

CHAPTER NINE - THE NEW RELATIONSHIP 85

What does a "new relationship" actually mean? 87

When they say that it's all in your head 90

When new and old relationships collide 91

Letting go, closure, moving on, and acceptance...in context 93

Conclusion - The Unexpected Gifts of Grief 94

The gifts 95

Never the last words 97

♥

AUTHOR'S NOTE

I make no claims to being an "expert." I am not a certified counselor, psychologist, psychiatrist, or doctor; my views are my own. I am just a normal person, a mom, a daughter, a business owner, a friend, who has walked—and in some ways, will always be walking—the path through grief. I want to share how I best harnessed it and worked on it, in hopes of helping others do the same.

– Alexandra

♥

CHAPTER ONE
UNDEFINING GRIEF

WHAT YOU ALREADY KNOW

There is an unwritten rule that in the first chapter of any book on grief, the author must explain what grief is—as if the readers of the book don't know.

Grief affects everyone at some point. We reach out for guides like this, not for definition, but for reassurance, companionship, answers. We may already be going through life's hardest tests. Our grief affects our every waking moment—and every sleeping moment—and ruthlessly changes us from the inside out.

We absolutely know what grief is.

Out of nowhere, when I was only thirty-one years old, I lost my husband, Mike, to a sudden tragedy. Mike was thirty-nine—a young man still—and our children were only four and six. That man was and is my soulmate. To this day, I am gratified for having known and loved him. And losing him was a blow that almost leveled me. Within a matter of hours, I went from being a happy wife to being a widow. I was in a state of shock—nothing had prepared me to lose someone so close to me.

At that time, I had dealt with loss before, but none had so mercilessly turned my life upside down. I was shocked to the core, unable to process the truth until days—maybe weeks—later. Then I found myself coping with not only my grief but our children's as well. I was trying to run a business at the time and had multiple responsibilities and roles. Some days I felt like hiding in bed, but I simply could not—too many others relied on me. The road from that time to now was a long and complex one, full of discoveries—some painful, some remarkable—that I want to share with you. I write this book for anyone who has suffered a loss. Your grief experience is yours alone, but you need not be alone in living with it.

For my part, I discovered that many of the resources about grief focused on people at different stages in their lives than my own. We read about grief to learn if—and how—others survived it, that we're not alone, and that we are seen. Maybe that what we're feeling is "normal" because, otherwise, it feels so utterly abnormal. We want the strange comfort of knowing that someone else has been through this. We want to know if there is any relief from it. If we'll ever be the same again. If someday we will once more recognize ourselves or the world, assuming there comes a time when we're able to look again and learn how to be OK.

As humans, we respond to loss with grief, which is not a singular state of being but a complicated process involving a tidal wave of different emotions, unlimited causes, unspecified amounts of time, infinite methods of coping or not coping, and it comes in combination with input from a society that surrounds us and the beliefs we were raised with and the personality we have developed.

Grief is recognized as painful, yet maybe we can find beauty so powerful that our hearts can break all over again. Grief is a wholly unique experience and yet somehow also universal, because grief is not one thing. It is everything that comes when we deal with significant loss, and a significant loss is usually part of a significant life.

The most brutal grief process seems to happen when we lose a loved one; this is the experience that shakes us to our foundations.

We grieve for many reasons. We may grieve the loss of a job, a change in status, the end of a marriage, rejection, infertility, addiction, a missed chance, a failed business, body changes, imprisonment, or a child's leaving home. We grieve losses that affect us directly and indirectly, and maybe a change in the world itself might cause this feeling. We may grieve without fully realizing it. It's a process that happens with or without our consent. *Anything* we lose or do not gain that is personally significant, the loss of which disrupts our feeling of stability and safety in life may cause us to grieve.

Mourning, a term that goes hand in hand with grief, is sometimes used interchangeably with it. Mourning and grief are not the same, however. Grief is what happens inside us, in our thoughts and minds; mourning is an external expression and has to do with our behaviors, our "outward" illustration of the anguish we feel. Mourning is what we do during the grief process. We mourn when we perform rituals or talk to others about what we have lost. Mourning is a companion to grief and can help us with the internal processing of our emotions.

Symptoms of grief are somewhat easier to pinpoint than the definition of the process, though still not concrete. People who are grieving may experience the following symptoms with varying degrees of intensity:

1. **A sense of the "dangerous unknown."** Part of the terror of grief is that it can often feel alien, and you don't know what to do about it. You've never been through something like this before.

2. **Lack of energy.** Even the ordinary activities of life feel impossibly strenuous. You can't believe the amount of effort it takes just to get dressed, take a shower, or drive somewhere. Just speaking with other people feels like more work than you can bear.

3. **Loss of interest** in things you used to care about. And, in fact, the things you used to care about may seem frivolous and ridiculous. You may wonder

how you ever wasted your time on such stupid distractions.

4. **Sleep disruption.** You may sleep more, less, at different times, have night terrors, or find you can only sleep on a rug on the floor or curl up in front of the television set.

5. **Eating disruption.** Whether you stop eating or can't stop eating, whether you gain or lose weight, whether you're craving weird foods or can't stand the thought of swallowing, you're not eating the way you did before.

6. **Weakened immune system, and increased pain.** You're suddenly hurting all over, and you catch everything. There are several causes for this (disrupted sleep and eating habits are just the beginning), but it doesn't change the fact that you feel awful. If you're prone to migraines, you'll get more of them; if you have backaches, they'll get worse; if you tend to get bronchitis after a cold, you'll catch more colds, and contract bronchitis that goes on for weeks.

7. **Loss of a sense of control.** The world is unpredictable and frightening, and you have no control over it or yourself. It makes you want to hide under the bed and keep your loved ones under lock and key.

8. **Loss of focus.** Your mind drifts alarmingly. You forget things you've never forgotten before. You screw up simple tasks, walk into rooms and don't know why you're there, and sit staring into space for half an hour without a solid thought materializing.

9. **Lack of confidence or self-esteem.** What's the point? You're a mess, feel terrible, and you have no

control over anything. Nobody wants to be around you. Life is mean and unfair, and you don't think you can handle it.

And those are just the major groups of symptoms. There are dozens more of these life-gobbling monsters that can slip into grief: feelings of hopelessness, isolation, anger, guilt, resentment, and even suicidal thoughts.

I'm not so cavalier as to say there is an end to grief or that everything will one day look just as it looked before. What I will tell you now is that grief is natural, normal, and survivable. No, your world will not be the same as before, nor will you. But it will be livable and recognizable, and you can inhabit it as a wiser and kinder soul.

In many ways, grief is a testament to the importance of what we lost. We do not grieve for things that never mattered to us. In my grief for the loss of my husband, I considered how lucky I was to have had such a love in my life. My grief moved me from unspeakable loss and despair to the desire to help: myself, my family, and others. That is why I wanted to write this book—to share what I have learned.

Am I "through" with the grief process? No, nor do I believe there is ever an end to it. I still have things to learn and steps to take. I still have times when depression and anger slip into my days, and that may never go away entirely. But I am leading a happy and productive life. I love being a mom to my kids, love my work, and I'm taking care of myself and my own needs. I am harnessing my grief so that I can work with it rather than fighting it.

STAGES OF GRIEF

In 1969, psychiatrist Elisabeth Kübler-Ross wrote the best-selling and highly influential book, *On Death and Dying: What the Dying Have to Teach Doctors, Nurses, Clergy, and Their Own Families*, in which she proposed her theory on the "five stages of grief." When she wrote about them, Kübler-Ross was talking about the stages experienced by the dying themselves, a theoretical framework that she developed from her extensive work with the terminally ill. These stages (sometimes called the Kübler-Ross Model) are now widely accepted as a guide for the adjustments we must make after loss, a general "human condition" experience that illustrates how we process life-altering changes.

The five stages—and I know you've heard of these before—follow. I'm going to give some examples of thoughts that *may* occur during these stages, but as is the case with human emotions, there are no absolutes.

10. **Denial:** *This is not happening. This is all a bad dream. Someone made a mistake. They are wrong.* Denial is a strange animal, a protective device our minds erect. Perhaps it gives us a buffer.

11. **Anger:** *Who or what is to blame? How dare God or the universe, or fat, or even the deceased do this to me? This isn't fair.* We commonly react to loss with anger, and why not? When something hurts us, it makes us furious and frustrated. We measure up our lives and say, "I have done nothing to deserve this."

12. **Bargaining:** *Maybe if I promise to live a better life, maybe if I sacrifice something, maybe if I do good deeds, things will change. Can this loss be undone somehow if I say the magic words?* Bargaining is that human tendency to believe, even for a moment, that we might finagle a do-over or find an easier way out or somehow lessen our pain.

13. **Depression:** *This pain is unbearable; how can I escape it?* Depression is the stage that normally lasts

the longest. It's the hardest too. Here is where the real danger lies, because depression is so often a struggle *against* pain, and in our efforts to escape it, we may withdraw, isolate, turn to addictions, and, in dramatic cases, consider suicide.

Sometimes we can "make the turn" out of depression ourselves, rising from depression organically with time and reflection, and sometimes we cannot. In the stage of depression, it is vitally important to support connection and communication with others, with professionals, and with yourself. Doing so can ease your suffering while also ensuring that someone is looking out for you.

14. **Acceptance:** *I know this pain is bearable because I am bearing it. Life is different now, but it can continue. There can be happiness again. The loss has meaning, and I will make the best use of that meaning to help myself and others.* If you are in one of the earlier stages of grief, like anger or depression, "acceptance" may sound almost offensive. "How can I ever accept this loss? I refuse to accept it. I'll never accept it."

But that's not what it means. Acceptance never discounts the importance of your loss. If anything, it fully embraces that importance, in a way that honors the person or thing we have lost. Acceptance means different things to different people, as is the case with all the components of grief.

Since Kübler-Ross's 1969 book, extra or enhanced stages have been proposed, which is why now you will also hear about the "Seven Stages of Grief." Although, in all honesty, the more one talks about grief, the more stages seem to arise. Anyway, here are some more things that may or may not happen during grief.

"**Shock**" is now included as occurring alongside or just after "Denial." Shock is a fuzzy area of unreality where we may function in a daze, unable to fully comprehend the significance of the event that has just happened. It's another protective device that nature bestowed on us; in the wild, shock is meant to give animals the time and capacity to escape danger. Escaping from a lion is hard for a gazelle with a torn and bleeding leg unless shock is playing a part, dampening pain and blood loss, putting fear aside, and letting instinct take over. In human terms, our shock in response to tragedy may lead us to think, "This thing has happened, and I don't know what to feel or if I feel anything or what to do or what any of it means." Months or years later, you may not recollect the hours or days following a loss.

"**Guilt**" has been added as a stage. There's no sugarcoating it; this feeling is a complicated nightmare. It figures into almost every stage and it's so hard to shake and it's so hard to argue with. "If only I had. If only I hadn't. I should have said something, done something. I never. I always. *This is all my fault.*" We'll talk about this more in Chapter Four.

"**The Upward Turn**" sometimes refers to the lifting of depression as acceptance begins.

"**Reconstruction**" is how we put ourselves back together. Most of the time, it is listed alongside acceptance. Yet, I think reconstruction may begin the moment the loss happens, when we manage to take that first step forward, no matter how much we wish we did not have to do so.

"**Hope**" is listed alongside or after acceptance. This is a lovely word, and a lovely feeling; it is a balm to all suffering. Hope is powerful; you can have it even during the most awful moments. Hope keeps us going when nothing else will.

Kübler-Ross proposed a sixth stage to her model in later years called "**meaning**," at which point we find a place for our grief experience to matter in our lives, because in our transformation, we may learn and grow.

BEYOND THE FIVE STAGES

There has been considerable criticism of Kübler-Ross's model since the time she published it, but this is not because it is "wrong" so much as that it has been over-accepted as a defined road map of grief when, in fact, it was merely a way to explain and understand that grief has many faces and common threads. We like easy explanations, and there is no easier explanation than a checklist of to-do emotions.

The same problem has arisen because health organizations, such as the American Cancer Society, say that the grief cycle lasts "about a year," another widely misunderstood guesstimate, for lack of a better word.

We must always beware of mistaking a generalization as the standard operating procedure. When you hear that working through grief takes "about a year," this is not a sign that you'll be "all better" twelve months after a loss. What it means is that after about a year after a loss, if one's ability to function hasn't improved, if there hasn't been some progression toward reconstruction, it may be time to seek professional help.

And even that is still a generalization. There is no need to wait a year to see a therapist or a doctor if grief is overwhelming you, for example. And after a year, you have no obligation to be "back to normal" or "over it." (Ouch! Those are a couple of highly volatile phrases. We'll look at those and other things *never* to say to a grieving person in the section, "When people say the wrong thing.")

The key point to remember when discussing the stages of grief is that this is neither a uniform pattern nor a uniform order of events. These "stages" of grief can happen for five minutes or five months; they can happen at the same time, return, be skipped altogether, or occur completely out of order. If you endure more than one bout of grief in your life (and the truth is, most of us do), your experience may completely change. No two people will experience grief in the same way, and there is no "correct" way to experience grief. I think it's misleading to put grief on a continuum. But knowledge of the stages is pervasive in our society, and you can hardly discuss bereavement without someone mentioning a stage of grief.

"Well then," one might ask, "if the list is so unpredictable, what is the point of it?" A few reasons:

- It's easier to talk about grief when there are agreed-upon terms for its components. I can't put a meaningful dialogue out there without acknowledging what denial is and what depression means.

- It's helpful to be able to recognize what some of these components are as you experience them; this can ease that feeling of "the dangerous unknown" that is such a frightening part of grief.

- It may be comforting to know that at some point, acceptance and reconstruction can begin.

Those who study the psychology of grief have proposed some alternate theories; one came from the well-known 1982 work of William Worden, *Grief Counseling and Grief Therapy*. Worden's model, like Kübler-Ross's (and not incompatible with it either), is flexible and its steps may be repeated or revisited. His four steps, extremely simplified, are:

1. Accepting the reality of the loss.
2. Working through grief and pain.
3. Adjusting to a life without the deceased.
4. Finding a connection to the deceased while still moving forward.

The importance of that final step, that of forging a connection to the deceased, was also stressed by Klass, Silverman, and Nickman's 1996 study and the resulting book, *Continuing Bonds: New Understandings of Grief*, in which they suggested that forming a new relationship with a deceased person should be encouraged. I believe wholeheartedly in the benefit and comfort of this important step. This, too, will be the subject of Chapter Nine.

Remember, the "Five Stages of Grief" or the "Seven Stages of Grief" or any grief model that you read about is a description only, not a rule, not a rating system.

If you are thinking, "There are a hundred stages of grief and I'm suffering from eighty of them right now," you are not wrong. As we move forward, let's keep in mind that grief requires only two things: you and a significant loss.

Let's work forward from there.

♥

CHAPTER TWO
THE DEATH-DENYING CULTURE

I live in the United States. If you do as well, then you and I share a disadvantage when it comes to living with the grief of bereavement. We are surrounded by a society that would like to pretend death isn't real.

A "death-denying" culture considers discussion or dwelling on the death experience as impolite, uncomfortable, and awkward. We don't like to think or talk about death as an inevitability and encourage ideas promoting sustaining life, at all costs. We "fight" disease, we "battle" old age. We put such a strong value on life that death, despite being inevitable, becomes taboo. Often, we look upon death as a type of "giving up." When faced with the unpredictable nature of the world, we look for someone to blame (and often, someone to sue), and for protections and reasons why the same things will surely never happen to us. The possible causes and the prevention of death seem more important to us than the idea that someone has died.

Strangely, however, even as we distance ourselves from the concept of real death, we romanticize and obsess over the concept, unable to resist hearing tales of horror, murder, and mayhem. We rubberneck at other people's dramatic tragedies and fantasize about embracing and yet somehow cheating death. One might believe that we were all just delighted with the idea of dying, except that our notion of death is distant. It is a plot point, something that happens to somebody else. Death via natural causes doesn't get the same status as causes that are violent, unusual, or controversial either—how dreadful to think about the cardiac arrest or kidney failure! If death can't come dressed up as a screenplay gimmick, few of us can summon any interest until the issue lands on our doorstep.

Of course, we understand, but don't put much thought into the fact that we will someday die. "Someday" is decades away, and thinking about it too much surely must be unhealthy. Why would we ever want to dwell on something so depressing?

HABITS OF DEATH DENIAL

Here are some traits often found in death-denying cultures like ours:

We use euphemisms for death.

Look at us; we can barely say the word "dead" in its real context and meaning. Our loved ones aren't *dead*. They have "passed on," "passed away," "gone to a better place," are "six feet under," if we're feeling facetious. Maybe they are simply "no longer with us."

We may mislead children about death.

Talking to children about death is terrifying—for adults. We can't even deal with the concept ourselves, and now we must clumsily explain it to a wide-eyed little innocent. We sugarcoat as best we can when it's abstract or tell kids that it's not something they have to worry about. If death should occur, we're quick to pull out the euphemisms once more. Grandma is "in heaven," she's "gone to sleep," or "she's gone away on a long trip." Does that seem unlikely? Not at all. People will say astonishing things to avoid telling children the truth about death. We don't encourage follow-up questions and don't understand that our vague suggestions are even more confusing and frightening to the children we're trying to shield. (This is a big topic, so see Chapter Seven for more about parenting while grieving.)

We hide death away.

Morgues are in the hospital basement, so as not to remind patients that death might happen there. Terminal patients are often separated from society. Most people wish to die at home, yet as of 2018, according to the CDC, only 31 percent of deaths occurred at home, as opposed to 35.1 percent dying in hospital care and 26.8 percent in some form of long-term care[1]. Under most circumstances, we put the bodies of our deceased into someone else's hands as soon as possible for burial or cremation preparation, and we rarely see or take part in handling the body.

Our medical community focuses on prolonging life.

Death-denying seems to go hand in hand with advances in medical technology. By and large, the medical community wants to keep us alive for as long as possible, and we accept this as normal because we think of death as a failure. Even having advance directives (such as do-not-resuscitate orders) is not a guarantee that a person will be allowed to die. The cultural focus on cheating death may create dread and despair at the idea. This is not meant to disparage the amazing advances that science makes to help us lead healthy lives. But when we begin to see death as the enemy, we lose sight of the fact that a "healthy" life may also include a dignified and natural death.

We resist making end-of-life plans.

Although setting our affairs in order is one of the kindest and smartest things we can do for our families, many people resist doing so, unable to bear the thought of planning their death arrangements.

I should note that in the past few decades, some sections and aspects of our culture have begun reforming this type of thinking. Palliative and hospice care are far more accepted ideas than they were forty years ago. Colleges and medical

---

[1] https://www.cdc.gov/mmwr/volumes/69/wr/mm6919a4.htm

schools now include courses on death and dying. Conversations about death are encouraged, though they still must often be planned ahead of time[2]. Tonight, we will talk about death, presumably so we *don't* have to talk about it again for the next six months.

WHY IS DEATH DENIAL A PROBLEM?

During bereavement, you might find all this counterintuitive. You'd very much like a world without death. Why would you want to accept death, to embrace the idea of mortality? Right now, death is causing you some of the worst pain you've ever suffered.

The major problem with living in a death-denying culture is that death unavoidably happens. Those left behind must carry the weight of death on their shoulders for a time, while in the middle of a society that finds death just as distasteful as ever. There is no guarantee of a social support system in place to help us when we need help the most.

I experienced this myself. People do not know what to say to the bereaved. Terrified of saying the wrong thing, they often say nothing. They don't know how to help. They're afraid that we might cry or say something devastating. They cannot seem to wait for the moment when we will get "back to normal." Probably, they don't even want to be around us; this stuff might be catching. As a result, we (the bereaved) suffer increased isolation and feelings of strangeness, otherness, and a completely unfair demand to be done with grief long before we are ready to be.

Now, in all fairness, we don't do this to each other on purpose, not exactly. Most of us were raised this way, surrounded

---

[2] Schueths, April. "In the U.S., we live long, but die hard." March 9, 2016, Sociology in Focus. https://sociologyinfocus.com/in-the-u-s-we-live-long-but-die-hard-2/

from birth by people and institutions that avoid the subject of death. We have little or no training or preparation for what to do in the face of grief.

But, indeed, the United States and many "westernized" cultures have made it a long-standing practice to avoid thinking too hard about death, which can leave the members of that culture vulnerable and unprepared when it happens.

OTHER VIEWPOINTS FROM THE WORLD

The variety of ways that grief is expressed or not and the kaleidoscope of viewpoints on death is quite amazing. However, remember back in Chapter One, I warned about the danger of generalizing. So once again, let me just say that no one culture has completely "solved" grief, nor does any certain culture get it completely wrong either. Also, when I refer to cultures or faiths, we naturally understand that not all members may adhere to these practices. But let's look at how some cultures generally handle the concept of death and dying differently to see where we might be selling ourselves short on the grief process.

There may be months or years of death-related rituals.

Rituals can hold an important place in the grieving process, but our culture shies away from them, and we are long past the days when we wore black for a year or more to indicate mourning. We give ourselves a funeral, burial, or ceremony of some kind. We take two weeks off work, and then are expected (by ourselves and probably others) to sort of "pick up and continue" where we left off.

Other cultures embrace a lengthy post-mortem process, setting up rituals of remembrance, socializing, and life celebration long after a death has occurred.

For example, Judaism encourages death to be acknowledged and discussed openly by the community. After the burial process, the grieving members of the Jewish community do something to let the people around them know that he or she's been affected. They may wear a black armband or a black brooch and hang black crepe in their windows to illustrate that they and their house have been touched by grief. Jewish people have grieving stages for the type of relationship they had with those who died. Their sadness is thoroughly recognized and embraced; while undergoing their normal routines, the people in their communities treat them with respect and deference, and they're excused from customary activities.

Following a death in Japan, close family members gather to wash and dress the body for cremation. Shrines in their homes honor their ancestors and dead loved ones. For a year after bereavement, meals are still prepared and presented for the deceased, fostering a connection between the family and the perceived afterlife.

If we in the United States want further rituals, we must usually make them ourselves— and I strongly encourage you to do so. We'll talk about this further in Chapter Eight.

<u>Other cultures allow far more emotional and physical expression of grief.</u>

Few things cause us as much discomfort as witnessing genuine grief. Judging by the popularity of video footage of bad behavior, we have no trouble watching people in states of rage, drunkenness, or entitled misbehavior—and even tears and crying, when these things seem unjustified. But put us in a room with a person who is overcome with grief, and we're immediately scrambling for the door or at least looking for a way to change the subject. And if it's you who is overcome with grief? Culturally, we are terrified of crying in public. We excuse ourselves quickly, hide our faces, and run for privacy. Public displays of grief seem disruptive and awkward, as if we are imposing on those around us.

This is not so worldwide. Many cultures encourage expressive emotional wailing or gesticulations as a demonstration of the pain the bereaved suffer. In Egypt, they expect families of the departed to wail in agony in response to a loved one's departure, a loud emotional distress. Haitian cultures use ritual wailing, and upon the death of a loved one, people gather for a social event that lasts many days and utilizes chanting and dances to physically express their anguish.

Muslims believe that crying cleanses the soul, and open weeping is encouraged to express grief. After their burial process, there's a forty-day mourning process. There's even a tradition (though it is less commonly practiced now) in which mourners cease using all electric devices for those forty days, allowing time for introspection and meditation without distraction. After a death occurs, it's common and expected that one asks the deceased's family about what happened. Talking about death is a form of socializing therapy that can be cathartic.

<u>They stay spiritually connected to the deceased.</u>

Bolstered by our medical technology and a strong sense of cynicism and/or pessimism, we tend to argue ourselves out of some very comforting beliefs and practices. Our culture separates death from us, even when our hearts tell us the opposite is true; our culture encourages us to "break" our connections with the dead, even when our hearts refuse to do so.

We are a culture of explainers who can always find a logical reason for something. If you see or dream of the person who has died, you might be told that it's "all in your mind." If you set up a shrine, you may be accused of being "unable to let go." If you feel that your dead loved one is watching over you, you may be patted on the shoulder and told, "There, there," like a child who has just told a fairy tale.

The Day of the Dead, *Dia de los Muertos*, is observed by

Latino cultures all around the Americas. This is a three-day celebration when the bereaved take time to remember and honor the deceased, and while they accept the permanence of death, they also see this as a time when the dead may return to visit their friends and descendants. Survivors use the time to mourn, but they also celebrate. The event brings the entire family together to remember their heritage. Usually, shrines are created to include photos of the departed as well as offerings to make those departed feel as if their spirits can be at home and be welcome.

<u>They don't conceptually separate life and death.</u>

Westernized cultures think of life and death as linear events that are opposites. Death is the end, or worse, death is the result of sin. Christianity, the prominent religion in the United States and many other westernized cultures, has a bit of a double standard that is fixed in our cultural awareness. While Christians believe in a heavenly afterlife and reunification, they also consider death to be outside of God's plan. Death is a punishment for sin, says the Christian Bible, visited upon us when Adam and Eve committed the original sin. We forfeit the right to live forever because of evil actions, and death is the result. The very foundation of Christianity is that belief in Christ will save us from death[3]. We may have additional trouble reconciling with our faith when someone we love dies because, deep inside, we believe it is a punishment for something: something they did, something we did, *something* has gone wrong. We ask questions that are almost impossible to answer. "Why did this happen? Why was he/she taken from me? How could this be part of a divine plan? Couldn't a benevolent higher power prevent this?"

Two of our world's major religions are Buddhism, which has approximately 400 million followers, and Hinduism, which has around a billion followers. Neither of these religions sees

---

[3] https://www.britannica.com/science/death/Christianity

death as the opposite of life or the end of life. Buddhism has an intricate philosophy of life and rebirth. Our self is made up of matter and energy that can be reborn after death. Rebirth comes in countless forms as well. We set our own destinies, and karma plays a big part; to put it extremely simply, karma is a kind of universal rule that "what goes around comes around" eventually, in this life or the next. When one "version" of us ends, we reshape and are born again. The cycle continues until we attain enlightenment and reach the ethereal goal of nirvana.

Hindus also believe in karma. Their belief is that actions have a direct influence on our *atman* or self, the essence that connects you with the divine. This self is reborn into the world as well. Their afterlife isn't just one singular place; rather, they have a towered network or structure of places where the self can travel and learn. Their purpose is to seek oneness with the universe sufficient to attain their own idea of nirvana.

These beliefs may sound a little perplexing to a westernized way of thinking, particularly since I'm summing up complicated belief systems in mere paragraphs. Rather than conducting an "Intro to World Religions" class, I'm only giving a quick outline to illustrate that, depending on your cultural background, you might perceive death very differently than millions or billions of other people in the world.

Cultures and religions with beliefs in rebirth or reincarnation (Hinduism being a primary example) see life and death as circular, and death serves as a doorway to new experiences and existence. Now, that is not to say that they don't grieve losses, simply that they don't view death as punishment or as a "ceasing to exist." The acceptance of life and death as stages (and perhaps not even the *only* stages) of existence means that personally and culturally their fear of death is greatly diminished[4].

---

[4] Various practices referenced in this section were researched through the following: What We Can Learn from Other Cultures about Grief, Death,

MOVING TOWARD DEATH ACCEPTANCE

We can see that a death-denying culture can rob us of many comforts after bereavement. The opposite type of culture is a "death-accepting" culture. At first glance, that sounds troubling. Death acceptance does not mean that one thinks death is great and needs to be rushed toward without any heed for safety or responsibility; it's really just a viewpoint that death is not shameful, frightening, defeating, or even necessarily an end. Death is not a bogeyman. It doesn't lurk around, listening to make sure nobody mentions its name and punishing those who do.

Death acceptance means that support for bereavement is more readily available, among other things. Now, let's look at ways we can incorporate practices from the rest of the world into our outlooks.

How can one "accept" death? It won't happen overnight and, like any valuable insight, may take some time and effort. Begin by doing the following:

- Accept that physical death is inevitable and beyond your control. You need not spend every waking moment pondering the end of your existence, but do ponder it. It's going to happen. Sometimes the death of someone important will drive this point home to you like nothing else. Accepting that death is inevitable does not mean obsessing or panicking either. When you have accepted the reality of mortality, fear diminishes, perhaps even disappears, and you find yourself better able to focus on the important things in life. Thinking about and discussing death is, ironically, a way to increase the fullness of living.

and Rituals—YouTube; Grief, Mourning and Different Cultures-rituals, traditions, and behaviors after death. Do We Grieve—YouTube; The Cultural Diversity of Grief and Loss—YouTube; https://www.joincake.com/blog/how-different-cultures-deal-with-grief/

- Learn about death. Learn about other religious and cultural beliefs to see how many ways the world looks at death. Learn about what happens to a dying body. Learn what others have experienced. We fear the unknown; the more you learn, the easier acceptance becomes.

- Make your end-of-life plans. Not only is this an extremely thoughtful gesture for your family, saving them from making hard decisions or enduring difficult legal procedures following your death, but it also relieves you of a considerable burden of worry. Plan your funeral. Write your eulogy. I know it sounds morbid; that's because we're in a death-denying culture. When you take the time to think about what will happen when you die, you get the benefit of seeing what you still want to accomplish in life and what things you would like to put your focus on.

  After my husband, Mike, died, I realized the incredible value of making end-of-life arrangements. While I got my affairs in order, I also wrote a letter to my immediate family members to be opened when I pass. It was a personal letter they could have that expressed how much I care about them and our relationship.

- Feel, rather than fight, emotional pain. Thinking about our deaths might make us feel sad or fearful. Well, we spend a lot of time struggling not to feel painful emotions. We throw ourselves into activity, distraction, addiction, and doing whatever we can to keep ourselves from what we are certain is unbearable. Our brains are tricky, though. Usually the harder we deny our pain and fear, the harder those feelings come back to bite us, and if we don't allow their expression, they'll express in some other way: sickness, anger, bitterness, despair, hopelessness, withdrawal. When we take the time to sit with our emotions and simply let them be, what we discover is that these feelings are not the monsters we suspected. There is nuance and intelligence in sadness. Listen to what your heart is saying. Recognize the cause of your sadness and the importance of letting yourself experience it.

There is no switch we can simply turn on to move instantly from anxiety about death to acceptance. As much as it is a cultural phenomenon to separate death from life, it is also a personal one.

You choose whether you will dread or fear your death. Likewise, you are under no obligation to fear expressing, and living with, the grief that comes naturally with bereavement. Just understand that the culture around you has some catching up to do.

When you are grieving, the most helpful thing you can do for yourself and those around you is to express your needs aloud. In doing so, people know what they might do for you or understand when they need not do anything as our first impulse when we see pain is to try fixing it somehow. Most of the time, people around you want to help because they understand that under the same circumstances, they would want help too. Our society may be death-denying now; that is changing. We can promote that change from the inside so that bereavement no longer must be an isolating, embarrassing, or frightening experience.

♥

CHAPTER THREE
BEING THERE

At some point, we all grieve. And at some point, we all want to support someone who is grieving. In this chapter, we'll begin discussing how to provide support in the best way you can.

Much of the following advice will need to be adjusted depending on how well you know the grieving person. For example, you would probably go to far greater lengths to support an immediate member of your family than you would a co-worker or acquaintance. Also, you likely would be better prepared to know what a family member might need or want.

This is not to imply that you must gauge a relationship on a scale of 1-10 to determine just how helpful you should be. Every circumstance requires some adjustment, that's all. When you support someone who is grieving, whatever support you are willing to offer that the griever is willing to accept is a good thing.

Let's start with the first and most terrifying task:

WHAT TO SAY WHEN SOMEONE DIES

Oh wow. This is a doozy. We're living in a death-denying culture; few of us have a chance to learn anything about discussing death in a helpful way. Yet here we are, looking into the eyes of a devastated human being. Now what?

We don't know what to say, so we say anything. We're flummoxed and freaked out and the words come flying from us. "What a terrible, uh, tragedy. You look like you're holding up well. I just can't believe it. Call me if you need anything."

Then we bolt, shaking our heads, thinking, *I never want to do that again!*

We think we *must* speak. Most of us are uncomfortable with silence. When someone you know is grieving, geez, you've got to acknowledge it, right? And look at this mess: at funerals, we often push attendees into lines and *make* them face the bereaved, forcing everyone into a spotlight where no one wants to be. It simply screams, "Say something!" Here we go again. "What a beautiful ceremony. I'm so sorry for your loss. What a wonderful person he/she was." And then we bolt, again ...

By the way, none of those sentences were grotesquely wrong; at worst, they were just awkward and depersonalized. We *mean* well. Few of us go up to a grieving person to make them feel worse. And the truth is, your words will not make them feel worse. Your words will probably not make them feel better either. Chances are good that in five minutes, they won't remember what you said at all. They have other things on their mind.

Does this mean you can just say anything that pops into your head? No, but it does mean that you are not required to be eloquent or unforgettable.

Here is what you can say.

<u>If time is short (i.e., the funeral line):</u>

I'm so sorry. Express your real sorrow at the loss. If it was someone you also knew and cared for, say so. If you did not know the deceased, express your sorrow for the griever's loss.

I will think about you and/or pray for you. It is fine to express your intentions to keep people on your mind, and many people pray. Even if the griever does not pray, and you do, you can say it. But remember, thoughts and prayers only go so far. We'll talk about taking useful action later in the chapter.

<u>If you have more time:</u>

Would you like to talk about it? If they say yes, then listen. And this means attentive, nonjudgmental listening. It means letting them cry if they need to cry or laugh if they feel like laughing or rage if they feel angry. You're not there to edit their narrative. You offered to listen. Open your ears and let it happen. Remember these pointers:

- You cannot "fix their problem." It's tempting to try alleviating a grieving person's emotional anguish with platitudes and advice. Don't do this, because loss cannot be "fixed," and there is no "problem" to solve. This is grief, a natural, normal response that must be experienced. Don't try to cheer them up, don't start tossing out silver linings, and don't advise unless it is asked for or unless you think there is a real risk of personal harm, like the griever is having suicidal thoughts or engaging in destructive behavior.

- Empathize, but be careful not to make the conversation all about you. When empathizing with a loss, you might want to share your own experiences so that the griever feels seen and that they're not alone. They'll know they can share more details with you. This type of empathy can be helpful, but it needs to be steered in the direction of how your words relate to *their* experience and emotional state. It can be easy to get on a tangent about what happened to you and what you did in response.

- You don't have to provide answers. Grievers may ask some tough questions: "How can I live through this? What am I going to do?" It's not your job to know; they don't expect you to anyway. You can say "I don't know. But whatever happens, you can talk to me about it."

I'd like to help if I can. When people are hurting, we say things like, "If there's anything I can do, just let me know." Or perhaps, "Oh dear, is there anything I can do for you?" And we mean it, of course. The only problem is, we're a culture that doesn't like to ask for help, and someone experiencing grief may not know what they need. Making a "to-do" list is a bit more than they can handle right now. So, approach this proactively.

Actions speak louder than words. If you've ever gone through grief, think back to what helped you or what really would have helped if anyone had bothered. Then ask your griever directly if it would help them; if so, offer to do it. These are solid chores of everyday life that may simply overwhelm them right now. People often like to cook for the bereaved, figuring they won't feel like cooking for themselves. That's fine, but that's the easy one.

Offer to drive, to help answer emails, to clean, to make phone calls, to babysit, to grocery shop, to do laundry, to help do something with all those funeral plants. You may offer them a couple of options. "I can do A or B or both." Statements like this make them aware of what you're able to do, and they can specify a preference. Financial help is a delicate subject, so unless you know the person well, approach this with caution or confer with others. If it seems like a collection would be welcome and useful, it's a very generous thing to do.

Don't just offer at the funeral or during the first days after a death happens. Follow up. The death of a loved one can result in months of feeling exhausted and burdened by day-to-day activities. Far too often we expect people to bounce back from death and pick up their routines after only a few weeks.

And by the way, if you volunteer to do something, follow through. I hope that goes without saying.

WHAT NOT TO SAY WHEN SOMEONE IS GRIEVING – AND WHY

Have you heard these before? There are the old standards, offered repeatedly because they seem inoffensive or maybe upbeat. But they're not.

Here are some to avoid.

- **"They're in a better place."** *Really? Well, they're not here, and here is where I want them because I'm in a worse place without them.* And by the way, not everyone shares this belief.

- **"At least they lived for [*amount of time*], at least you had them for [*amount of time*]."** *Just how much time do you think is enough?* Avoid ticking off years on a calendar as a measure of some inexplicable reason to be grateful. Grief and love do not know time.

- **"Everything happens for a reason. God has a plan for everyone."** *What possible reason could there be to take my loved one away from me?* This is a bad time to get philosophical, bring up fate or destiny, or talk about how death might have been necessary for some grand ethereal plan.

- **"Time heals all wounds. Give it some time."** *This wound will never heal, I don't think I'm going to survive this, and even if I do, I'm not sure I want to heal anyway.* At present, time may terrify a griever. While their pain may seem endless, they may truly fear their feelings will change. And finally, it's quite dismissive, like saying, "I'll get back to you when you're past this rough patch and back to normal, OK?"

- **"Well, at least you still have [*blank*]."** *People are not interchangeable.* Never, never suggest to someone that they needn't feel as bereaved because they still have someone else.

- **"Just try and stay busy. Try not to think about it."** *I can't think about anything else. I don't want to think about anything else. Stay busy doing what? I can barely get out of bed in the mornings.* Trying to push difficult emotions aside is unhealthy physically and mentally.

- **"You have to stay strong. Stay strong for your [*blank*]. You're being so brave. Keep your chin up.** *What you mean is, don't make a scene, right?* Grievers need to express a lot of extreme emotions. If they're told that they're being strong or brave, it's usually when they're being calm, quiet, and unemotional. Saying that they need to be strong or brave means just about the same thing: don't get all emotional; it'll scare/upset someone else. These sorts of statements reaffirm to the griever that they can't show emotion, that sadness and anger are bad, and that they should bottle up these hard emotions as tight as they can.

- **"It's time for you to move on. It's time for you to let go."** *It's time for you to mind your own business.* We can only decide for ourselves when it's "time" for anything to happen in our hearts and minds. And the expressions "move on" and "let go" are problematic because they imply leaving someone behind.

- **"No way!" or worse, "You're kidding!"** *What? No, I'm not kidding—why would I kid about something this awful?* This is kind of a touchy subject.

We often express our dismay with euphemisms that undercut the seriousness of a situation, and "Oh, no way!" or "You're kidding" seem to be common ones right now. Here's the thing, these phrases sometimes just slip out. The grieving person may not give it a second thought, or it might sound hurtful to them. If you say something like this and think it was hurtful, apologize and tell the truth. "I'm sorry, I'm just so shocked. Of course, you're not kidding." But if you can help it at all, avoid exclamations that sound dismissive. "I just can't believe it," is a safer exclamation of the unreality of a tragedy.

- **"I understand exactly how you feel."** *Oh no, you don't. You can't possibly.* Take it easy with your empathy. Many of us have suffered grief, so yes, we can understand that it is confusing, frightening, painful, lonely, and sickening. However, grief is unique to everyone. When someone is truly hurting, don't diminish that hurt by saying that you've been there and done that. Use your experience to be a better supporter and listener, not to explain to them how their experience is going to play out.

SUPPORTING SOMEONE EXPERIENCING GRIEF

Now I'd like to offer some practical advice on supporting others when they are grieving, particularly when grieving the loss of a loved one.

Leave your expectations at the door. Grief is expressed differently by everyone, and anyone's expression of grief can change from day to day, even minute to minute. There is no schedule for grief. The bereaved person may seem to be doing quite well one week, and the next week falling apart. They may be in the mood to laugh and joke. They may be in the mood to throw things and shout in rage. Open your heart and your mind to whatever may come.

Don't be afraid to ask. If you ever feel unsure about what to do, what to ask, or say, just getting their preference might mean a world of difference. It never hurts to ask for permission when you're uncertain how an action will be received. For example, "I have a wonderful memory about your mother; may I share it?" The bereaved will likely be glad to know your thoughts, but if the bereaved says no, don't take it personally. They may be finding it hard to listen to others at the moment, no matter the subject.

Don't become another burden. We want so badly to help that we may overstep into the realm of being another thing the griever must take care of. For example, you may offer to "move in" for a while to help them take care of things or be a companion, but that will backfire if you become a houseguest they must feed, clean up after, and entertain. They have quite enough to deal with already; don't add to it by getting in the way. It's a fine line, but what this means is that if you're going to help, *help*. Practice some self-awareness about boundaries.

Don't underestimate silent companionship. We often feel uncomfortable with silence, but there's nothing wrong with it. Sitting beside someone, holding a hand, crying with them, even hugging are all fine ways to offer support, and you need to say nothing, with one exception, which is ...

Ask permission before touching. Unless you are very emotionally close to someone or know them very well, ask permission before initiating physical contact. It's all right to open your arms and ask, "Would you like me to hug you?" or "May I take your hand?" This is simply polite, first of all, but secondly, not everyone likes to be touched, especially when they are upset. If your offer is refused, once again, don't take it personally. Offer to just sit with them instead.

Use the name of their deceased loved one. Don't avoid saying the name of the person they've lost, or avoid acknowledging that there has been a loss. Sometimes we do this because we "don't like to remind them" of their pain. No, I promise you, they're already living with that knowledge at the forefront of their minds most of the time. You won't be reminding them of anything they haven't been thinking of all day long. Saying a loved one's name means that *you* remember too, and that is a comfort.

Check up on them at regular intervals. Ask the griever for a preferred time and a preferred frequency; the commitment will vary depending on how well you know each other and your proximity. For example, once a week at a specific time, make contact, even if it's just a text or email. Better yet, call them. Visit in person, if you both agree to it. A scheduled, regular check-in is good for many reasons: namely, it reminds the bereaved that they have support, and it gives you the chance to extend extra help if it is needed. Remember, *you* do the checking. Bereaved people can forget things, lose track of time, and isolate themselves. It is all right to give your number and say, "Call me if you need anything," but that's fairly vague, and they probably won't feel comfortable about bothering you. So, you must take the initiative on this.

THE GRACE PERIOD

A friend of mine finds human psychology fascinating, and she's been through bereavement herself a few times. She proposed to me that during those first difficult days or weeks, the shock-and-denial period of grief, there should be a grace period where we forgive ourselves and everybody else for saying "the wrong thing." As I stated earlier, when we start talking, we're probably trying to make things better, or at least not make them any worse. But words come out wrong or get taken the wrong way because emotions are high and unpredictable.

So, let's try giving ourselves a grace period. If you are the bereaved, forgive people who may speak awkwardly or say something inappropriate. If you are the speaker, do your best, but don't feel you must avoid speaking altogether or that you should distance yourself because you feel like you misspoke. This is a time for more communication, not less.

Remember that we're all only human. Always treat a griever like a person, but one whose whole world has been turned upside down. Be gentle, be respectful, and just be there. Kindness and compassion are treasures. We never forget the special bonds that we forge when we reach out in times of tragedy to support each other.

♥

CHAPTER FOUR
GUILT, BLAME, AND ANGER

BUT FIRST … SHOCK, DENIAL, AND UNREALITY

When looking at a list of the stages of grief, we see a consensus that when we experience traumatic loss, we first encounter shock and/or denial. Like all grief stages, there is no pre-ordained amount of time or level of severity for these states of being, and like all grief stages, aspects of shock and denial may return at different points in the process.

I considered writing an entire chapter about shock and denial and then realized something. People in shock or denial probably aren't the ones reaching out for guidance. No, it's when shock and denial have worn down—to return only in fits and spurts if they return at all—that we're faced with the phases of grief that may hurt, confuse, and enrage us, the ones that make time feel like an enemy, that make life feel so much heavier than it should. Then we reach out. If you have reached out by reading this book, then I'm glad you are seeking help and I hope that my words can bring you some kind of relief.

Shock and denial are worth discussing, but I won't go into great depth. These are instinctive responses that your brain engages in when you feel threatened. They are a kind of cushion. Once they wear off, you may wish they were back again.

My husband died suddenly and unexpectedly. When the news of his death came to me, I reeled from the unreality. How was it possible? We were just having a conversation a few hours before, and now he was gone!? The days that followed

36

felt surreal and fuzzy. I remember time dragging but also flying by. I could not form a coherent thought or concentrate for more than a moment.

Intellectually, I understood what had happened. It's not as if I thought someone was lying to me or there had been a mistake. I had to share the news with our children, after all. I had to repeat those words to other people who loved him. I got it.

It just didn't stick. I kept thinking Mike would walk through the door any minute, or that I might wake up to find him there with me. I couldn't comprehend a world where he didn't exist. It was as if a split had happened in the universe: some version of Mike had died, but my Mike was fine because it wasn't possible for him to be gone. Here I stood in the house we shared with our kids, and I was eager to tell him about this terrible news because I shared everything with him. "Something awful has happened, Mike," I would say, as soon as I could see him. "Someone has died." And he would make me feel better and safer.

"No, wait," I would think. "Mike has died. I can't tell him about it because he's the one who is gone."

Yet, five minutes later, I'd be listening for the door again, expecting that at any moment, he might walk through.

Of course, shock and/or denial can happen even when you're expecting the trauma. Your loved one may have been sick for months or years. You might have seen your tragedy coming for a long time. It's still a loss. It will still take time to adjust: a major part of your life has changed, and a person of importance will not return.

Are brief moments of "forgetting" also a form of denial or shock, or is it as simple as a habit? When we have traumatic losses, we may have moments when we manage to forget. Something distracts us. Maybe our consciousness stalls a bit when we awake each morning. There may be a moment when everything seems normal again, like nothing has changed.

In those first months after Mike's death, I often came out

of sleep to lie in bed for a few blissful seconds, just expecting to hear him moving around in the house.

Met with silence, it would hit me once more.

Whatever lightness we felt in those forgetful moments disappears and the weight descends again. We don't want to forget. We don't want to deny it. But we can admit that those forgetful moments are rather easier than the ones that follow...

GUILT

Guilt is a slippery, clever beast. It sneaks up and attacks us, a cruel emotion that can be inflicted from the inside and out. Here are just some of the things that guilt can make us think about:

- **This is all my fault.** Even if it was utterly impossible, you'll find a way to blame yourself. Your guilt will construct incredible scenarios to support the belief that this was all your fault.

- **I should have been a better [*blank*].** Whatever relationship you had, you believe suddenly that you weren't good enough, and your loved one died having been neglected somehow. This can stretch back over the course of a whole lifetime. Things like, "I was a terrible child. I never gave a good Christmas gift. I was too preoccupied. I didn't call when I should have. I didn't visit enough. I worked too many hours." You'll look back and see yourself as some kind of villain and you'll forget every good thing you ever did.

- **The last thing I said (or did) was [*whatever it was, it feels like the wrong thing*].** We aren't poets 24/7. We aren't even pleasant 24/7. So, whatever was happening, guilt will tell you that your loved one died with your horrible or wasted words ringing in their ears.

- **If only I had [*done something differently*].** This one is awful. Because in some ways, it seems so obviously true. When accidents happen, for example, one can quite clearly see the chain of events that led to them. So yes, you can really dig down into this one and convince yourself: if you had done something different, the outcome might have changed.

- **I'm so angry I could scream, and it's wrong to be angry.** Anger, especially when it's directed toward your deceased loved one, can feel like a betrayal of everything they meant to you. Thus, more guilt.

We'll discuss ways to cope with all these thoughts.

BLAME

As if guilt isn't hard enough, it comes with blame, because while we're busy feeling *our* responsibility for a tragedy, we consider the ways we believe that *others* were responsible. Blame has all the earmarks of guilt except that it is directed outward.

Along with accusations of this nature comes victim-blaming, when we or others identify a person's faults that led to their death. These can be rational, "Well, he smoked three packs a day for twenty years," or they can be irrational, "Well, he shouldn't have been standing there," or anywhere in between. Victim-blaming is about self-defense; something inside us insists that identifying a cause, especially one we think was preventable, might keep tragedy from happening to us.

Be careful with this. You are also feeling guilty, angry, exhausted, and overwhelmed, a time when speaking your mind without any filtering gets too easy.

Grief is not a free pass to abuse others, and few of us are so beyond the pale of grief that we can't see our inappropriate behavior coming. The aftermath of a death is an unfair time to start airing grievances about past transgressions or slights. Blaming each other for causing a tragedy or at least failing to prevent one is no more helpful than blaming ourselves. When we are in pain, it is important to accept that pain. Acknowledge what is causing it, and even speak to others about it, but let's draw a line here. I recommend keeping these accusations to yourself or talking about them to a neutral party, such as a therapist, who can help you distinguish rationality from irrationality.

Sometimes we grieve alongside others who—thanks to their pain, guilt, anger, or denial—decide to push blame in our direction. They may say some astonishingly hurtful things. "If you had only paid more attention. If you had only been there. If you hadn't made that mistake. You could have stopped this. Why didn't you do something? How could you let this happen? You were neglectful. You were selfish."

I'm not sure it helps much to say so, but it's very likely that these accusatory remarks toward you or the deceased are made to mask and subvert the speaker's feelings of guilt and anger. In their effort to reconcile death and escape their pain, others may choose to put you or the deceased in their crosshairs. How you react to statements like this is a matter of personal choice. In the last chapter, I mentioned allowing a "grace period" during which people are forgiven and forgiving of the things that are said when coping with terrible loss. Forgiveness is a powerful tool, though not an easy one.

You are, however, permitted to defend yourself. Don't start fights about it—everyone is already fragile enough, and this situation can quickly devolve into terrible things being said. I do think you should make it clear that you won't put up with it. "I understand you are hurting, but blaming me won't help.

I don't appreciate it. I'm already in enough pain. We should support each other, not turn on each other." If the person in question won't let it go and insists on targeting you, you may remove yourself from their presence and stay removed until both you and they can cope better with the pain of loss.

I'm sorry to say that some people are not mature or aware enough to ever stop blaming others for misfortune. If several months or even years have passed and you still feel like you are being blamed or singled out as responsible somehow, there is a problem, regardless of whether you are projecting or whether you are really a target. When the death of a loved one threatens the foundation of a relationship, you may:

- Seek outside help or counseling.

- Confront the issue to find out the truth.

- Decide you can live with it because the blamer doesn't know any better and you can forgive them for it.

- Or, sever the relationship. That is sad; it is another loss to deal with. Maintaining connections with our lost loved ones is important, and shared friends or family members serve as vital connections. But no one needs to remain in a situation where they feel abused.

WHAT USE IS GUILT OR BLAME?

The real bite here is that guilt and blame do serve a purpose in our efforts to cope.

Guilt and blame are our ways of putting the world in order. When bad things happen, we want to find a reason, something or someone at fault, something to repair so this tragedy won't happen again, or some way to say, "It won't happen to me." The idea that life is unpredictable, that the universe doesn't have any concept of "fair play," is so difficult to accept that we purposely look for all the things that could have prevented our loss and then say, "Well, if only ..."

Now, take a deep breath, and hear me out. Along those same lines, guilt can also be a way of overestimating our power and importance. If we can find ways to blame ourselves or shortchange our performance in a relationship, we can view ourselves as vital, influential beings. "I had the power to make him happy, but I failed. I had the power to change the outcome, but I didn't. My behavior was integral to this person's existence."

That's too much. No one has that kind of responsibility or skill. It's sort of unpleasantly gratifying to believe it, though, especially when we are grieving. As you experience these feelings, remember that your importance and influence in the lives of others have their limitations:

- We cannot control the thoughts and actions of others.

- We cannot control the universe.

- And, every event that happens is the result of the interplay of infinite causes—nothing ever happens for a single reason. The universe is far too complex for that.

"BUT YOU HAVE NOTHING TO FEEL GUILTY ABOUT."

So, here's the thing. If you talk to someone and tell them that guilt is eating at you, they will probably try to talk you out of it. "There's nothing you could have done." And, "You have no reason to feel guilty," and "You shouldn't feel that way, you were a wonderful blah blah blah ..." You may bristle at their comments, or heck, you may agree with them. It doesn't matter; guilt still gnaws at your thoughts. *I could have changed things somehow.*

Grief counselors recommend that we not say things like this because telling people not to feel guilty is another way of minimizing their emotional experience. When people feel guilty, we should at least acknowledge that guilt is a normal part of grief.

But some people will say it anyway, so try to be forgiving of their efforts. Guilt is a terrible burden, and they don't want you to live with it.

ANGER

After Mike died, I went through periods of seething anger. I felt anger toward God, fate, and the rest of humanity. I was angry at society for not understanding my pain. I was angry at impositions on my grief, but also angry at the grief itself. I was angry at Mike for leaving me. I was angry at myself for letting him leave.

Anger and guilt are tied closely together. Being angry at a dead person can worsen our guilt. We're trained never to speak ill of the dead, so it's hard to express our anger aloud. We feel guilty already, then we get angry, and then we feel more guilty, then we can't talk about it, so we get angrier, so we feel more guilty. The words "vicious cycle" come to mind.

You know what I'm going to say. "Experience your anger. Accept it as normal. It's OK to be angry."

"But it's so stupid to be angry at someone for dying!" you might argue, even as you feel angry at someone who has died. Especially if it was someone you loved dearly, your mind says, "How dare you be angry? You loved this person! It's not right."

It may feel wrong, but it's so very ordinary and expected. We don't get angry about things we don't care about. We get angry when things that we need and love are threatened or removed or damaged. Just watching someone you love put themself at risk is enough to make us furious.

Just like other emotional experiences, talking about or writing down your reasons for anger may help you see the real source of your feelings. Anger often rears up in response to fear. We fear things like pain, isolation, and change, which are three prominent outcomes of losing someone you love. Let yourself be angry about it. It's OK.

While we're on the subject, it's OK not to be angry too. My friend Britt had a difficult conversation after a close friend of her group committed suicide. She felt terrible sadness and loss but no anger toward the friend, because he was mentally ill. The others in the group told her she was angry, and she had every right to be; she said, "No, I'm not angry at him. I'm only so sorry he saw no other option." They said, "You are angry; anger is a normal response," and she said, "I'm not angry." They said, "You're denying your anger," and Britt said, "I'm not angry at him but I'm starting to get angry at *you*," and then things became heated. Anger, like any other response to grief, doesn't have rules or requirements.

COPING WITH GUILT

Guilt, and the blame and anger that may come with it, must settle on its own; it may never settle entirely. Humans will probably go on blaming themselves for things forever. It is programmed into us, often by our upbringing and religion. We hear it in church, and we watch our parents do it to themselves, and occasionally guilt is thrust upon us by others—it's a classic tool of manipulation.

However, you will hopefully begin to rethink your perceptions. There are a few things that might help you achieve a new balance in how you view your responsibility for a tragic event. So, as guilt continues to linger—or sit squarely on your weary shoulders—consider the following:

- **Acknowledge that you feel guilty**, then acknowledge that most grieving people feel guilty, that it's normal, and that it's OK. "You say that about all these feelings, Alexandra," you're telling me. I know. But it's true. Don't fight or deny your emotions; that always makes things harder.

- **Examine your guilt**. Explain it aloud to someone or write it down. Look at the logic. Examine if your guilt is rational or irrational. Are you demanding things of yourself that are almost impossible? Now, either way, don't dismiss it. Irrational guilt doesn't care that it's irrational. Just know the difference. Besides, saying or writing your feelings can alleviate their pain.

- **Imagine what the object of your guilt would say**. If you had the chance to tell your loved one about your guilt, your responsibility, your terrible behavior, neglect, last words, whatever it is, if you could tell them, how would they respond?

- **Counter your feelings of guilt with direct evidence to the contrary**. When you consider the source of your guilt, you may be able to find concrete proof of the opposite. "I was a bad daughter," you might be thinking, "because I didn't visit enough." Is that the case? Were you often in contact with Mom or Dad? Did you have a close relationship even though distance separated you? Make a list, real or mental, and remind yourself of these things when that guilty thought sneaks back at you.

LEARNING FROM GUILT

An important step in living with grief is learning from it; our guilt can be a powerful teacher. If you wish you had been a better friend or relation, be one now to the people who remain. If you wish you had said, "I love you," more often, start saying it. If your guilt and the blame and/or anger that comes with it have a "resolution" or response that is gratifying to you and others, do it. Each time you behave more kindly, responsibly, or lovingly, thank your lost loved one for helping you recognize this lesson and for the happiness these new experiences bring.

♥

CHAPTER FIVE
WHEN YOU NEED HELP

In this brief chapter, let's talk about when it is appropriate for you to reach out for help and support during the grief process. The answer is ALWAYS. We should always, always, always reach out for help and support when we grieve.

Yes, but it's not that simple, is it? Look at us!

- We don't like to ask for help.

- We don't want to look weak.

- We don't want to bother anyone.

- We don't know who to ask, anyway.

- We're pretty busy ... lots to do ... work, kids ...

- We're surrounded by a culture that wants us to "suck it up" and get better quickly.

- We don't know what we need.

- We don't believe that help is even possible. We think that nothing will make this better!

And grief is just terrible sometimes. You didn't know that anything could hurt this much and for this long. So, it's going to continue being terrible no matter what, right? When you're in the middle of your biggest heartbreak, feeling bad every single day is kind of the norm. We forget what it is like to be relieved of the burden of grief. When do we draw the line? At some point, I hope you can recognize your need and say, "Oh wait a minute, I'm actually not doing so well on my own, and I really need help." Let's talk about this.

WHEN TO REACH OUT

If I'm being honest, I believe you should reach out as soon as possible. After a tragedy strikes, we should immediately connect ourselves with our loved ones, friends, and support networks, and keep that connection strong for as long as it takes. I think everyone should ask for and have as much support as they can get.

Nevertheless, I also know that things aren't always so cut-and-dried. Weeks after a crisis, our support networks may have cut off or at least dwindled away. You might feel bad for pushing your burdens onto other people when they have lives to live too. We may push ourselves too quickly forward. We have obligations to meet, children who need us, salaries to earn. At some point, you may discover that you're in over your head.

So, do two things. Ask for help and accept help when it is offered. For example:

When you think you need it. I know that sounds *so* obvious. Remember, however, that during the grief process, you may forget what is ordinarily obvious. You may doubt yourself and your decisions. Don't. Ask for help sooner rather than later. You deserve it.

When someone else says you need it. If your best friend, close relative, or someone you've known for years, says, "I'm worried about you and I think you should talk to someone," be willing to accept that they might know what they're talking about. They're not saying this to be cruel or dismissive. They're genuinely concerned, and if they are this involved, they may be able to help you find a therapist or support group, get you to an appointment, or otherwise assist with what is difficult for you at this moment.

When you are unable or unwilling to care for yourself. Major depression comes with feelings of worthlessness and anger, and for some reason, our reaction is to punish ourselves more. If you are neglecting things like eating, sleeping, showering, social interactions, and your basic safety (like simply taking your prescriptions or keeping warm), these are warning signs. This is a difficult call because your first instinct will be to do nothing for yourself. You feel helpless and defeated. What's the point of trying? View yourself with a bit of distance to see what is actually true. Are there moments during the days when you think, "What is happening to me? I didn't used to be this way." Listen to that voice.

When you are self-medicating to escape. Excessive drinking, drugs, and/or substance abuse are means of escape from pain, and they obviously harm you. These things do not "fix" your grief; they only numb it and put it at a distance while putting you and perhaps others at risk.

When you seriously consider harming yourself or someone else. Grieving people can have these thoughts: maybe things would be easier if I just gave up or maybe if I died too, I could join my loved one again. And anyone undergoing the difficulty of grief might think, "I'd really rather just not wake up tomorrow." So no, "thinking" is not the same as "doing," but if these are more than just fleeting thoughts or your "what if" starts becoming a "how to" plan (that is, you are hoarding pills, buying a gun, giving away all your personal property, disassociating yourself from your life), do not hesitate for a single moment to ask for help. Please reach out, and if you reach out to someone who doesn't take your thoughts seriously, reach out to someone else. In the United States, 988 is the Suicide and Crisis Lifeline; you can call or text with someone immediately.

This book is about harnessing grief. The truth of severe depression could be an entire book unto itself. If you're suffering that intensely, please seek professional help. You have a right to ease your suffering in a positive way, loving yourself *and* what you have lost.

WHAT HELP IS AVAILABLE?

There's actually a lot of help to be found, even in our death-denying culture. You may not agree with all of these methods, which is fine. You should work within your own beliefs and comfort.

See the doctor. This is an easy first step. Go to your general practitioner and tell them what is happening. Doctors understand grief's devastating impact on our well-being. First and foremost, a doctor can find out if you're physically in any trouble. The stress of grief can be a genuine threat to your health. Next, a doctor can give you referrals and information about affordable support. They may be able to prescribe a medication if that is your wish, which leads us to ...

Medication. This is an extremely personal choice that must be made between you and your physician or psychiatrist. There are arguments for and against the use of medication when it comes to grief, and there can be a wide gulf between the two sides. Some people feel it's no better than drowning your sorrows in whiskey; others feel that a prescription was the turning point that let them begin to heal. I believe medication is a legitimate option, especially when combined with therapy. Medication cannot cure grief, no matter what, so don't expect a miracle. What a medication can do is improve your ability to cope and move forward. Medications don't work the same way for everyone, so it's important to do this correctly. Follow doctors' orders and make all your follow-up appointments.

Find a support group. Participation in a group of people who have undergone a similar situation and who now have a common purpose can be a great relief. Support groups help alleviate anxiety, loneliness, and depression. You receive the benefit of hindsight from members who have been on your journey, and they can supply even more ideas for support. Here's an interesting "tip" on choosing support groups, because so many groups are now accessible in an online format.

Look for a group that has something *else* in common with you, in addition to grief and/or bereavement. For example, I could join a support group for parents of young children. Or I could consider one for entrepreneurs who must cope with grief while dealing with the stressors of running a new business. Support groups form among all types of people: those who share hobbies, backgrounds, and careers. The benefit is that you are there for each other's grief, but you also share a piece of your ongoing life. This gives you a nice balance of support, which is why you are there.

See a grief therapist. There are people trained to help in this particular circumstance. When you're choosing such a therapist, remember that therapy is for *your* benefit. Decide what you want from it and if a particular therapist can give it to you. You need not continue seeing someone who doesn't help you or who makes you feel uncomfortable. We live in an exciting age of opportunity when it comes to therapy because now sessions can be conducted online. There is nothing wrong with face-to-face meetings and you may prefer them, but they are not always an option. If you live in a rural area, for example, your access to grief therapists may be quite limited. As long as you have internet access, you can reach out to grief therapists anywhere. This gives you an incredible number of choices, and you can base your choice of therapist on their methodology, beliefs, other patient recommendations, cultural knowledge, or any other aspect you choose. Medical insurance often covers grief therapy. If this is not an option, some therapists also include sliding-scale payments.

Tell people what you need. Once again, your friends and family want to help you, but they might need a hint about what to do. Most of the time, it really is a matter of letting them know that you need a shoulder to cry on, an ear to listen, or some companionship during a hard day. Other times, especially if you are unable to take care of yourself or decide what to do, the people who love you can get you the help you require. This is not a time to be "strong and silent" or avoid "being a burden." When things get to be too much for you to handle on your own, *say something.*

Look for spiritual guidance. In whatever form you choose, spiritual guidance can provide a lot of comfort. In the United States, one of the first groups we reach out to is our church group because these people know us well already and have like-minded beliefs, so they can provide both social and spiritual support. I spent many days in church after Mike's death, praying and seeking guidance there.

There is a catch here, though, and you may already be ahead of me on this. Talking about spirituality means something different for everyone. For some of us, spirituality is inexorably tied to religion. For others, the two have little or nothing to do with each other.

If you have spent your life in a particular faith or with a set of beliefs, severe grief can make you question those beliefs. You might suddenly be filled with doubt, for grief is a serious challenge to spirituality of almost any kind. When we invest ourselves in a belief system, we may also believe it will protect us from tragedy, sickness, or pain. And when it doesn't, we feel betrayed. Accepting that a higher power is "looking out for you" when things go so wrong, well, it's really hard to do.

I feel that religious faith can afford to be questioned, though, and there is nothing wrong with asking. The problem only arises when doubting your faith leads to feelings of guilt or shame, and you're already dealing with enough. Worse still is if other members of your faith cannot bear to listen to your questions. If at any point your faith-based support group starts to make you feel like you are wrong, sinning, or failing somehow, this is a sign to distance yourself from that. You need the space to explore *all* of your thoughts, not just the ones approved by the people around you. You need to heal both emotionally *and* spiritually.

There are other spiritual choices, too, and I don't personally believe they are incompatible with each other. You might seek training for meditation, breath work, homeopathy, sensory therapies, yoga, or the traditional medicines of various cultures. I found a powerfully helpful solution by consulting a medium who could put me in contact with Mike's spirit, a topic I will cover carefully in the next chapter.

CONCLUSION

Do you feel wrong about asking for help? Why is that? Is it because you don't think you're good enough? That you're not strong? Are you worried about what other people might think? If you're struggling on your own, you probably have a hundred reasons why you haven't gotten help yet.

But as someone who's gone through a similar tragedy, I want to share this with you. I thought the same things for a while, then realized I couldn't be good for anyone else until I was good to myself. I needed help and I finally reached out. I'm so glad that I did; the difference was profound. There are so many people who will gladly help those in need.

♥

CHAPTER SIX
CONSULTING A MEDIUM

This chapter is about my experience with a controversial subject. Over the past year, I have conducted twenty-two sessions with a medium to communicate with my deceased husband.

I can imagine more than a few reactions to this information.

You might support and agree with the idea, thinking things like, "You're so fortunate to have made this important contact!" and, "Of course, that's what I did too!"

Or, "What a wonderful idea; how can I try it myself?" "How do I take this step? Is such communication really possible?"

Or perhaps, you feel consulting a medium is a harmless but mostly useless endeavor: "Wow, what a waste of money and time," or "Well, if it makes you feel better, fine, but such things aren't real or valid."

Or, you might think, "Alexandra, you're treading on dangerous ground. This is nothing to mess around with."

And there's still another possibility: "You poor thing, you've been duped. You're the victim of a scam to take advantage of your vulnerability."

I'm saying these things now because I want you to know that I'm perfectly aware of the gamut of reactions to this information. So is my medium, my trusted friend and mentor, Maryann. She worked closely with me on writing this chapter. For that, and a multitude of other things, I thank her.

I'm not including this chapter to convince you of something you cannot believe or to talk you into doing something that frightens or worries you. From the beginning, we've proceeded with the understanding that your grief process is yours alone, and you must do what is right for *you* in order to navigate the journey. That being said, however, this is also my story to share. My work with Maryann is a key component. Even if you're unsure about using mediums, maybe I can show you how one person coped with some very complicated feelings, the same feelings you might be experiencing. Maybe I can help put those feelings into words and show how what might seem like a radical, or at least unconventional, method of coping did me so much good.

Please, read on with an open mind and an open heart.

HOW IT STARTED

I lost Mike so suddenly that my life was full of uncertainties and unanswered questions. Of course, I missed him, but more than that, I desperately wanted to speak with him. I'd try anything to grasp a sensation of closure, something that I could process with my feelings. Often, I felt like Mike was still around, reaching out to me. Like he still existed in some way that I couldn't quite reach back to just beyond my sight or understanding. I wondered if I was simply unable to grasp his permanent absence, or if maybe there really was something to the idea that departed loved ones remain near us. But I wasn't sure how to cement that connection. I did a lot of thinking and reading on how to cope with this feeling and my studies kept steering me back to the spiritual.

I approached Maryann Kelly of Intuitive Services Insight[5].

Maryann walked away from a very successful thirty-three-

---

[5] If you'd like to see some examples, Maryann has both written and video testimonials on her website at https://intuitiveservicesinsight.com. This might give you a good idea if the process is right for you. The site also comes with recommended readings and other medium resources. According to Maryann's website, she works "... *to bring peace, comfort, and closure to clients seeking communications with passed-over loved ones, (people or pets)."*

year career which included global responsibilities in IT, financial services, healthcare and benefit administration to follow her path doing mediumship and energy work. Her story intrigued me; her career path seemed like an excellent set of credentials. Because of my own entrepreneurial career, I felt that we had some important things in common.

Seeking the services of a medium is exactly like seeking the services of any professional helper, be it a doctor, lawyer, therapist, or pet-sitter. Do your research. Listen to trusted recommendations and investigate the professional's methods and beliefs. You want to find someone with whom you feel comfortable. Transparency and confidence matter.

When you speak with a medium, look for validation of information. Maryann, via her mediumship role, was indeed able to offer answers which resonated with me due to the unique detail specific to my husband and our circumstances. Had she not been in contact with Mike, she could not have known the details she presented to me.

DESCRIBING A SESSION

If you've never had an actual session with a medium, you might imagine our meetings taking place in an eerie room beyond a curtain of beads, seated at a small, round table under a purple tablecloth, with a glowing crystal ball under a dim light—and sure, we've all seen those TV shows and movies.

But that wasn't the reality. Maryann and I actually met online, over Zoom. According to Maryann, spirits can be contacted from anywhere. It's common for mediums to help people over a long distance. Spatial distance has no real effect on our connection to the other side. During our sessions, we maintained a quiet atmosphere without interruptions.

Maryann was kind enough to describe the process of her work for the book. The sessions she conducts are quite different from a seance. In a seance, spirits are requested. Maryann instead feels spirits who want to be with us, those who are already near us, and who are never too far away from our lives.

Spirits exist on the "other side." This other side has many names, but most call it the afterlife or heaven. Spirits on this other side can communicate with us through energy if we are open to it. Love is a powerful energy. Some cultures readily believe that the energy of love and our connections with the deceased can transcend even death, and this is what allows us to be close to those who have passed. Maryann can tap into that energy. She described it as a quantum field that constantly vibrates throughout the world. With the right amount of patience and acceptance, this field can be accessed. Anyone can tap into the energy that our loved ones send us; doing so means recognizing your intuition and interpreting that universal energy.

In Mike's style and demeanor, Maryann communicated precise information from my husband relevant to what was happening with me, my home, my business, and my children. Her work repeatedly validated that she was absolutely communicating with Mike, but more importantly, it also confirmed just how present Mike's spirit was in my daily life, as well as that of our children. It was a surreal, wonderful, and deeply emotional experience.

Of course, I asked how Mike was doing. I asked if I could communicate with him too, if he could see me, what he was thinking about, and what lay beyond death. I had so many questions. I didn't even know where to begin. That was part of the reason that I had so many sessions, though the reassurance and connection were far more important. Our work together boiled down to the thing that mattered most to me: Mike is still with us and always will be. The peace this brings to my heart is priceless. These encounters have been such a comfort to me. And, if you're feeling a little skeptical, I assure you that I was the one who initiated having additional sessions. Maryann never tried to either sell me additional sessions, pressure me, or take advantage of my vulnerable situation. She is extremely ethical and respectful. She considers her work sacred, and I agree with her.

Did our sessions provide me with what I sought? Yes. I got closure on some pivotal questions. I learned how Mike was doing and about the role he fulfills for me and the children, from the other side. I will always cherish Mike, but I am now able to move forward, which was important for me and of paramount importance for my family.

QUESTIONS YOU MAY HAVE

The idea of a session to communicate with your loved one might excite or worry you or raise many doubts and immense curiosity. I provide here some questions that might occur to you, and Maryann was kind enough to respond.

How do mediums help with the process of communicating between realms of existence?
By raising our vibrational frequency to connect with clients' loved ones and then passing along the information sent.

Do mediums hear the voice of the deceased?
Sometimes. It depends upon what message is sent.

Will I be able to hear the voice of my loved one?
Again, sometimes, if voice-related information is sent, and if the recipient can receive it.

What happens if you cannot contact them?
It's important to be open to the messages sent by the spirits who do come. It's not up to us as to which spirit comes. The more we are open to who comes, the better the chance that we will receive the information we need.

Remember, too, that what we need may be different from what we want. Finally, we can ask to try connecting later if the desired spirit does not come through.

What questions can I ask?
You can ask anything.

Can spirits predict the future or foresee events?
Possibly, but keep in mind that our free will here changes the trajectory of future events on a continuous basis.

TV and movies often make psychic work look quite painful and frightening. Does it hurt you to make contact?
No. I am focused on receiving information which comes very fast. The language of energy is indeed another language that takes time to understand.

What if my loved one is angry with me?
Spirits state the truth. Spirits do not seek revenge or to be hurtful. Recipients have a responsibility as to how they receive the truth.

What information would I have to give a medium so they can work?
It's not so much giving information as it is being open to receiving the information that comes.

Is this a good idea for everyone?
If someone only wants to hear from very specific spirits and only wants to hear certain specific information, then this type of session may not set optimal expectations.

How do I respond to people who say I am wasting my money and that this kind of stuff isn't real or may even laugh at me for trying this?

Stand in your own truth and follow your individual guidance as to what is right for you.

Is this an occult practice?
No.

Is seeking the help of a medium compatible with Christianity?
Yes, although others may feel differently.

How do I deal with new relationships if I'm still in contact with my deceased partner?
Deceased partners want their loved ones to be happy, as is consistent with unconditional love, so if the new relationship is in their best interest, great. If the new relationship is not in their best interest, information about this may be shared. Again, spirits state the truth and are not out to be possessive or hurtful. Recipients have a responsibility as to how they receive the truth.

What kinds of things do clients usually want to say to or ask of their loved ones?
How are they? What happened at the time of their passing? They ask assorted questions related to obtaining closure. They want to know that their loved ones are safe and in a state that is free of pain and fear. They want to tell their lost loved ones that they are still loved, missed, and remembered.

Do you think spirits can connect with people without the help of a medium? If so, how might they do it?
Yes. The short answer is that you can practice quieting your mind and be open to what comes without changing the information. Dreams, thoughts, and manifestations might be ways that a loved one would try to connect, but they are certainly not the only ways.

Do clients come to you reporting a belief that their dead loved ones are trying to reach out and tell them something?
Sometimes, yes.

What kinds of signs might one notice if a loved one is trying to make a connection?
Seeing symbols, words, colors, specific items, specific animals; hearing sounds; prevalence of smells; occurrence or recurrence of events.

I'm afraid of being scammed. Are there any red-flag behaviors to watch out for?
A disreputable medium, like any disreputable provider, is someone who does not have your best interests at heart. So, as in any such relationship, a manipulative person might try to make you feel insecure or that you need them. They might try to control you. They could be pushy in insisting you buy items or that they come to your home.

CONCLUSION

I include my experience with a medium because speaking to my husband through Maryann has been an integral piece of *my* grief process. It has been my own way of forming a "new" relationship, a topic we'll cover in depth in Chapter Nine. For me, this contact has made a huge difference. When we confront grief, we confront many things we "can't" do. I can't go back; I can't change what happened; I can't rush my healing or my feelings; I can't know the answers; I can't fix it; I can't, can't, can't have what I want.

For this piece of my healing process, it was finally, "I can."

I can speak to Mike again. I can know where he is and that he is all right. I can know he is with me, and I can move forward with that knowledge. I can believe in something greater than an ending.

♥

CHAPTER SEVEN
THE GRIEVING PARENT

When I lost my husband, I also lost my partner in parenting, and my children lost their dad. They were ages four and six at the time, so they were old enough to understand the loss, that Daddy was gone, but still too young to process death as a permanent thing. They had so many questions and so many concerns. For them, the impact was twofold because a parent was gone, and I was changed, thrown into a state of shock and grief that they could sense.

Grieving as a family is painful and comforting at the same time. While we can share memories and support each other, we might also find ourselves neglecting personal feelings (I lost my husband and best friend) by focusing exclusively on our children's pain (this family lost its father figure, and my children lost their dad).

Parents cannot bear to watch their children hurt. We want so much to have all the answers and fix all their problems. My intuitive little ones could pick up easily on my tumultuous emotional state. I tried to focus on them: upholding their schedules, assuring them that we'd be all right. I think my reaction was typical, but I'm not sure it was the best thing for me. It took me some time to realize that I couldn't be good for anyone if I wasn't good for myself.

HOW CHILDREN OF DIFFERENT AGES PERCEIVE DEATH

These are approximations. Some children will grasp abstract concepts (like "forever") sooner than others, and some children will be slower to understand. Media can present some confusing information—as death is often impermanent in cartoons and video games—but the major factor in how children react to death is in how their guardians/parents react to it. If they are raised in an environment that fears and dreads death, they will react the same way.

1. **Infants.** Babies have no concept of death. Regardless, they can and will miss an absent loved one. They can also sense sadness and grief in those around them and react with fear, confusion, or anger to changes in their schedules or the emotional withdrawal of a caretaker who is grieving. Babies as young as eight months will call out for, or search for, the "missing" person.

2. **Toddlers.** Death still doesn't mean much to them; they don't yet understand permanence. They have strong attachments to loved ones, however, and they are well attuned to the moods of their family. The difference between infants and toddlers is one of communication: they can more specifically communicate that they are afraid or angry. But patience is required. One may have to explain to a toddler repeatedly that their relative, friend, or pet is not returning because they continue to expect a reappearance. Schedules will be disrupted; that's almost inevitable, and toddlers don't react well to that. Well, adults don't either, if you think about it. Be understanding about their confusion. Expressing your grief in front of them is all right. "Mama is crying because she feels very sad." Toddlers love unconditionally; if you remain loving and nurturing, they will cope alongside you during all the difficult days.

3. **Preschool.** At this point, children are beginning to grasp death as a concept, but still not its permanence. Children of this age will have a lot of questions and will want to know why and how deaths occur. Because they still view the world from only their perspective, they may assume deaths occur because of something they said or did and that the resulting sadness is also their fault. They will want to know how the death will affect them personally, too, and may ask questions about that. Children at this age take things quite literally, so it is important not to use euphemisms for death.

   Common threads for infants, toddlers, and preschool children experiencing a loss include sleep disruptions, lack of appetite, separation anxiety, and reversion to old behaviors (for little ones, it can be things like regressing in toilet training or language skills). Anxiety, lack of sleep, lack of appetite—sounds familiar, doesn't it? These symptoms can also occur in older children and even adults because some things about grief are fairly universal. But in the case of your small children, who cannot describe their emotions or feelings, it is important to recognize that they can undergo the same disruptions. They are normal reactions—they're not easy—but they are normal and like many components of grief should ease over time.

4. **School-age.** From about the ages five through seven, children are old enough to understand permanence and the idea that all living things will eventually die. They may perceive death as an entity, like an angel, a ghost, or a "grim reaper." They remain extremely curious about the mechanics of death, like what happens to bodies after they are buried,

and they experience fear of the unknown. Children can still have a strong belief in magical thinking during this time and are imaginative enough to fill in the blanks of things they have not been told, making up their answers. As they become increasingly aware of the inevitability of death, they also may worry about their health and safety and that of their loved ones.

5. **Teens.** Teens understand mortality and death, but the traditional teen attitude is one of defiance. They know death happens, but often feel they are personally immune to it. They may become quite angry with a person who dies, feign an uncaring attitude, openly challenge the views and beliefs that others have about death, and have strong behavioral and personality changes while they adjust to the ideas of death. Teens don't typically like asking for support, even when they need it. However, don't assume automatically that a teen will behave this way; again, each child will have a different experience. Some teens may take over an "adult" role in the family if their parents/guardians are absent physically or emotionally, adopting a heavy load of responsibility. Teens can be a tremendous support in this time, too, as long as we remember to listen and communicate without judgment.

WHAT CAN PARENTS DO FOR GRIEVING CHILDREN?

The guidelines for dealing with grieving children are not so different from those dealing with grieving adults. Mainly, it is important to listen without judgment and without preconceived notions about what a person should or should not feel.

As the parent or guardian of a child, chances are fairly good that you know the best way to communicate based on their personality and age, as long as you remember that communication about death is difficult for many of us, so some extra effort may be required.

With that in mind, here are some guidelines to work with:

- Use simple words to explain, and be prepared to explain more than once.

- Based on the child's age, judge what details you may wish to leave out. You don't have to explain the full range of an illness or an accident to a small child. Older children (school-age, for example) can let you know how much information they are comfortable with processing by the nature of their questions.

- Tell the truth, without using too many euphemisms. Don't substitute terms like "gone to sleep," as a substitute for the reality of death.

- You may tell children the equivalent of "time heals all wounds." I recommended not saying this to adults, but this is a little different. When children first experience grief for a loss, they need to know that the intensity of this sadness will fade and that they will be able to feel happy again. Children don't grasp time in the same way we do, so for them, this is an acceptable and necessary comfort.

- Remember that questions may continue long after the death or tragedy. Children go through shock and denial too; it may be days or weeks before they begin asking for more information. As children age, they gain insights that may prompt questions even years later.

- Let them know what's going to happen. If a service or ritual is planned, let them know what will happen there and why. If they are old enough to understand, explain if schedules will be changed or disrupted. If visitors are coming, or if you all must travel, fill them in. Children are always at the mercy of the adults that surround them, and we often expect them to simply tag along behind us. Things are confusing, and the upheaval can be terrifying for little ones.

- When we explain that "everything living will die," children infer the obvious: that they will die and that you will die. There's no need to emphasize the complete unpredictability of life at this point. The truth is that most people live long lives; we take care of ourselves (we visit our doctors) and practice safety (like using car seats and seat belts).

- You may let children know your beliefs about the afterlife. For example, "Grandma died, but I believe that her spirit has gone to heaven," but be prepared to answer the follow-up questions, such as: Where is heaven? How did Grandma get to heaven if she was buried or cremated? What happens there? Who else is there? Can we visit her there? Will you go to heaven? Will I go to heaven? And so on.

- If talking about death or tragedy makes you uncomfortable, a child will probably pick up on it. It is all right to admit your discomfort. You may say, "Talking about death is hard for me because I'm not used to it, but I'll do the best I can to explain. Maybe you can help me."

- Let them ask all the questions they have. No question is intended to be disrespectful or silly. You may learn something yourself.

- If you are also grieving, say so, without shame. Cry if you need to, and cry with your child. Talking about your emotions, such as anger, with acceptance will help them understand that their feelings are normal and OK to experience.

- Children who still believe in magical thinking may blame themselves very specifically for tragedies. "Did Grandma die because I yelled at her?" Now, when we discussed guilt in Chapter Four, we said to allow people to feel their guilt without telling them the feeling is wrong. In the case of magical thinking, however, you may refute the logic. "I know you feel bad. But yelling or getting angry at someone cannot kill them, no matter how loud or mad you get."

- Children have an innocent, egocentric view of the world, which is perfectly natural because it takes some maturity to learn that there are other viewpoints and experiences outside of their own. A grieving child may want to know how death or tragedy will affect them personally. They may ask, "Who will read to me?" or "Where will we go for Christmas?" or even "Who will take care of me?" Reassuring them that they will continue to be loved and cared for is important. If there was a ritual performed by the deceased loved one (such as a bedtime story or a special day of the year), this ritual can continue to remember and celebrate that person's life.

- Permit laughter and play. Kids work out a lot of their questions and emotions through playing. And laughter does us all good. It's OK if something is funny, OK to see the humor in a situation, and OK to experience happiness, even during the saddest times.

- Remembering the loss aloud—whether the loss was a person, a pet, or something like a move to another town that left your child feeling adrift—acknowledges our feelings as valid. Say the names, remember what was important, and be willing to discuss good times and bad.

- Don't be surprised or dismayed by behavior changes. These may show up in all kinds of ways: regressions into more childish behaviors, flaring tempers, increased crying, nightmares, dropping grades, withdrawal, moodiness, and even outright rebellion. When behavioral issues arise, talk about them first. Keep rules in place, such as, "We're not allowed to hurt ourselves or other people. We're not going to get away with lying, stealing or scaring anybody," but pick your battles about the little things. Remember that your nerves may be just as frayed. Not every incident needs to become a "teachable moment." Sometimes it's OK to say, "Hey, it's been a rotten day, hasn't it? Let's just call it a scratch and try again tomorrow."

TAKING CARE OF YOURSELF

This is one I had to learn too. I was so concerned about my children's grief and recovery that I failed to process my own. I had a business to run, children to protect, and obligations to meet, but I also needed to take care of myself.

While the grief process has no set timeline and no set playbook, it nevertheless will run its course in everyone. You must give yourself the chance to feel your feelings. It is so tempting to divert yourself with other matters, and our children are a prime diversion; they need us, we love them, and their pain is ours.

Finally, you do not have to respond perfectly to this situation. Good Lord, don't put yourself under that kind of pressure. Just remember that you, too, have suffered a loss. You have a right and a need to grieve from *your* perspective.

Self-care doesn't have to be complicated or expensive. This practice is really about giving yourself some time to think, reflect, or even just zone out if that's what you want to do. You *should not* do any of these activities if they feel unpleasant, burdensome, or depleting. I don't want you to give yourself another chore. Self-care is about doing something that replenishes you. You have every right to experience pleasant, happy moments too; never feel guilty for alleviating your burdens.

Here are some ways to care for yourself, even while caring for a family.

- Get outside for a walk on your own, day or night. Walking in the moonlight can be as soothing as sunlight. Get some fresh air and a bit of nature; it's free and the benefits are many.

- If you can't leave the kids alone, take mental breaks by putting on headphones to listen to the music of your choice. Music is a significant emotional experience and, depending on your choice, can provide a variety of effects, so let yourself experiment with what works best—and you are permitted to enjoy the experience. You may choose to listen to songs that trigger memories, songs that energize you, songs that distract you, or neutral, soothing music that just lets your thoughts drift.

- Play with your pet. Snuggle your cat. Tussle with your dog. Pets are pretty in tune with our emotions, and they love unconditionally. Bask in that; it's worth it!

- Journal your experience. I wrote a letter to Mike each day after his passing, and it helped me get out my thoughts and feelings as if I was speaking right to him.

- Join a support group or groups, as nothing says you are limited to only one. The online community can be a big help here if you can't or don't want to leave the kids. Find a group for parents in your situation, for example. That can be quite a relief.

- Call someone to talk about anything. Obviously, it is good to talk about your feelings and your loss, but sometimes if you just want to dish about movies or fashion or the nonsense down at the office, that's OK too. Just have a grown-up conversation with another grown-up.

- Read for entertainment or information.

- Exercise or meditate indoors or outdoors. You know what works for you; just take the time to do it.

- Create something. Paint, write, compose, sculpt, cook. Start a new hobby, rekindle an old hobby, or keep up with your favorite hobby. It's OK to enjoy yourself, and creativity is a wonderful expression of pain *and* joy; it is a celebration of both life and enduring love.

You may have noticed that many of these are activities that parents are encouraged to do regularly anyway because nobody can be "just a mom" 24/7. But when we are grieving, it's easy to forget "normal" activities that bring us comfort. We may forget that self-care is even an option. We may feel like we don't deserve self-care or that self-care is simply selfish. Caring for yourself, however, is essential to caring for your family.

WHEN TO SEEK PROFESSIONAL GRIEF COUNSELING FOR CHILDREN

Grief therapy is an opportunity to address emotions with a neutral party, with someone who has knowledge and expertise in helping others through similar circumstances. Therapy is a personal choice. If your child has experienced a loss, you may choose to enroll them in therapy immediately, and that's fine if the child is comfortable with it.

Parents know their children and most of the time know when a problem has reached a point where outside help may be of use. Experiencing a loss is difficult and may result in disruptions of all types; the thing is that, generally, we can expect improvement over time. When we struggle with that improvement, we seek help. It is the same for our kids. Some signs to watch for, which indicate that it may be time for outside help, include:

- Chronic health problems
- Behavioral issues that do not abate or improve with time
- Persistent suicidal thoughts, plans, or fantasies
- Withdrawal that fails to improve, and even worsens
- Sleep disruptions (nightmares) that persist

If you want to get professional counseling for your child but are concerned about the cost, you might start with your child's school. Speaking with the school counselor can be a great way to access psychological services, some of which may be free or at least offered on a sliding-fee scale. Your child's primary care physician could also be a good source of information. There are a surprising number of resources available, including bereavement play groups and recommended reading for all ages. You and your child need not do this alone.

You may attend therapy sessions with your child; expect that sometimes you will be included in the session, and other times you may not be, to give your child some "parent-free" time to vent or express themselves.

HEALING TOGETHER

One of the best things about a family is our ability to share an experience and come through it together. Isolation and loneliness are some of the more difficult aspects of grieving; grieving with your family can go quite a long way to easing those burdens. In the next chapter, we will look at the importance of rituals and remembrance and talk about many ways that you and your kids can cherish and celebrate those we have lost.

♥

CHAPTER EIGHT
RITUALS THAT HONOR
AND REMEMBER

While you cope with loss, you may find it useful to make certain activities into rituals, which can happen daily, annually, or anything in-between, depending on how complex the activity is. A ritual is technically a ceremony with a series of actions performed in a certain order. We need not be quite that formal about it; rituals can be as simple as daily activities that hold meaning for you, allowing you time to reflect and experience your emotions in their fullness.

Why are rituals important to us? Rituals serve the purpose of comforting you and others while maintaining a connection with the one you lost. They honor all aspects of the relationship: you, the one you lost, and the connection that you still have with them.

Rituals have a beautiful component of timelessness as well; they encompass past, present, and future and remind us that even when things change, some connections cannot be broken.

IDEAS FOR INSPIRATION

I'm going to share examples and ideas for rituals, but you are free to do what feels right and appropriate. These activities may be done alone or shared with friends, family, and children. Your grief process will want solitude sometimes. On other occasions, a gathering is the perfect recipe for honoring and remembering our loved ones.

I'd only like to remind you that others may not be on the same wavelength as you. They may not wish to participate or may not see the benefit of the ritual; they may have their rituals or processes. The Golden Rule applies here: treat others as you'd want to be treated.

For example, if you are in a situation where you want people to contribute stories, memories, or special thoughts about a deceased loved one, make this voluntary, and be prepared to offer your own to begin with. Some people hate speaking to a group or may not feel ready to speak about the loss; you don't want to make them feel uncomfortable or unhappy. And when memories, stories, or thoughts are contributed, accept any emotions that come with them. Gatherings for remembrance must make room for a spectrum of feelings.

<u>Visit sites of importance.</u>

There are special places where we can feel close to someone who has died. The meaning of these places may be so profound that you can't bear the thought of going there without your loved one, and you may feel that way for some time after a loss. When you are ready, visiting these places can be comforting, and you may feel a powerful connection while you are there. Some people speak with their deceased loved ones while there. They may leave mementos and reflect on happy and meaningful moments. You may choose to visit alone, to be with your thoughts, or bring with you others who can share in the memories and feelings. This can be a one-time visit or a regular occurrence.

You know the places that are special in this relationship. Here are a few examples:

- **The burial site.** Some people find burial sites to be important markers and may, for example, bring flowers on Memorial Day, a grave blanket at the holidays, or other significant anniversaries. It's a time of reflection and honoring the dead.

Be aware that burial sites can stir some differences in opinions and attitudes. In the United States, cemeteries and other burial sites have taken on some pop-culture meanings: they are considered haunted, cursed, or spooky, and not taken seriously. You may find that older generations put much more importance on graves, headstones, and other markers than younger generations do; likewise, certain religions are quite specific about the handling of bodies after death. Some people do not find burial sites to have any connection to their loved one: they see the body as an earthly shell and the personality, spirit, or soul as separate, and while they believe a grave site should be respected, it is not a place of memory to them. As always, you must do what feels right for you, but don't be shocked or hurt if others do not regard a burial site in quite the same way you do.

If your loved one was cremated and the ashes scattered, you may visit that site; if you kept the ashes, you may bring the urn with you to a special place or simply sit with it in your own home as you revisit memories.

- **Special places you shared with the deceased**. Most relationships include "special" spots—a favorite view, restaurant, park, museum, beach, theater, church—or a location that perhaps you visited only once but was highly important, such as a vacation spot or the site of an important event like a wedding or marriage proposal. If these special places are difficult to visit (for example, in another country, many hours away from you, or perhaps no longer in existence), you can still "visit" them in your mind, with pictures, or by writing down the experience so that you can read about it again.

- **Special places that you always meant to go, even if you didn't get a chance.** Mike and I always planned to take a trip to the ocean in Florida, where he used to fish. I went there with his mother, and we sprinkled some of his ashes in the ocean with one of his close friends. I felt such a deep connection to him then and knew he was with us as we stood gazing outward. It was not an easy trip to take, but I treasure having done it and think of that spot often, revisiting it in my mind.

The giveaway ritual

This one is all about generosity and tribute, and it can happen within days of a loss, several months, or even a year later.

This ritual invites families or groups to come together and share items that were meaningful in the relationship. The terms of the sharing are up to you; it could be that everyone has something to contribute, or you might be giving out several items to people who were close. When items are given or exchanged, givers explain their significance. Some very ordinary things can become truly special when sentimental memory is attached.

A variation on this is to allow friends and loved ones to name a thing they would like to have. For example, if they shared a love of building things, they might ask for tools or supplies from the loved one's collection. Maybe after attending an event together, they both bought T-shirts, and they'd like to have that as a memento. Discovering what items hold precious memories can be an amazing revelation.

If you are asked to give something that you cannot bear to part with, be honest about it. If you ask someone for an item that they cannot bear to give you, be understanding.

Create a memorial in your home.

Whether you lived with the deceased or not, you may create a memorial of special things that connected you to them. This may take the form of a shelf of mementos, a photo album, a collage of pictures, a scrapbook, a slideshow, a flower garden, or a statue or marker. Your creativity and knowledge of the loved one will show you the way. If a single item is all you need, so be it; a single photograph might suffice. But if you want to devote a whole wall to the project, that's OK too. It can be permanent or temporary. There are numerous cultures in which altars are the norm, and certain things are expected to be there, such as special foods or arrangements. If you want to borrow those ideas, you may find them inspiring or you may create your own.

Once you have created a memorial, use it as a touchstone for a ritualized remembrance. You might light a candle each day and think about your loved one or burn a stick of sage, traditionally a cleansing, peaceful gesture that promotes restfulness for spirits.

Write (or record) letters, journal entries, and stories

As I've mentioned, I wrote many letters to Mike after he died. One of the many difficulties of losing someone is all the things left unsaid—well, this is your chance to say them. We can speak to our loved ones too, but getting these things recorded permanently has its advantages and the ritualization is a big part of this. First, a daily writing or recording session is a helpful ritual in itself. Later, however, your work will continue to flourish as a memorial and testament to the person you love. You may revisit your work later and get a better handle on what you're feeling.

If you've asked questions, you may find the answers you seek, thanks to your wisdom or the assistance of others. You may even receive an answer from your loved one through a sign, dream, or message. Answers come to you in the form you expect. When I say that, you may think it sounds like wishful thinking. What it means is that your mind will be as open as you allow and will interpret things according to your beliefs. There is no "wrong" way to do this.

<u>Carry a token or memento</u>

If your loved one had a favorite article of clothing or jewelry or something small enough to carry on your person, it can be a comfort to wear or carry it. You always have a physical token with you, something you can hold in your hands and touch throughout the day. You might consider it a charm or protection, a link to their spirit, a focal point for a brief meditation, or a reminder that your love continues. I wear Mike's wedding ring as a necklace and I also had a ring made from some of his ashes and a piece of sea glass that he gave me. These tokens keep him close to my heart.

Children love tokens. We all know how much they enjoy wearing their hats, baubles, or clothing that belongs to someone they adore. I wouldn't recommend letting them wear Grandma's diamond wedding ring; it's best to give them something that can take the rigors (and forgetfulness) of childhood and can be easily replaced with a similar item if it is lost. Scarves, costume jewelry, coins, keys, or little collected items are fine. Did Grandma collect matchbooks, marbles, or postcards? Photographs or written notes are also wonderful and easy tokens to carry.

<u>Meals</u>

Food is a major family connection and a centerpiece to most of life's events. For this ritual, it's as simple as providing your loved one's favorite dish or dessert in honor of them. Say ahead of time that you're making it because it was a favorite. Make it with all the love you feel, and enjoy it as much as they would have. If this is a group event, folks can be asked to share stories or memories if they would like to—and share the recipe, too! Now your loved one's favorite can become someone else's.

Some people also like to set a place for their loved one at the table, a ritual that is fairly common worldwide.

Anniversary gatherings

You may have annual gatherings on special days, like wedding anniversaries, birthdays, or a time of year that your loved one found very special. If you feel it is appropriate, you may mark the anniversary of their death; this will likely be a time when your own emotions are unpredictable and you might like the company and support. But this is entirely a personal decision.

Such gatherings can be lively celebrations or simple affairs. Adapt the scale to your own level of energy and capabilities; there is no need to throw a lavish, complicated party if you don't feel up to it. And be patient with others; they may not really know how to respond to an invitation to a party in honor of someone who has died. In our death-denying culture, we're all feeling our way along toward a new understanding and acceptance.

Plants and flowers

If you enjoy gardening, planting something in honor of your loved one is a wonderful memento that adds new life to the world. Flowers, trees, even a vegetable patch. Choose something that they loved, like their favorite flower or tree, or choose something that symbolizes love for you, such as roses. Or research the "traditional" meanings of flowers and plants from around the world. There is a lot of surprising trivia on the meanings of herbs, blooms, and plants of all types.

As these living things are cared for, we can remember our loved one and celebrate this new beauty that we add to the world in their honor.

Entertainment

You and your loved one likely shared some kind of favorite entertainment, like music, movies, TV shows, books, or games. You can make this part of a new ritual by which you enjoy these things once more and remember the good times you had together.

I know that sometimes it is painful to think of doing those activities without your loved one. You may feel like your enjoyment of them has been ruined. Don't push yourself too hard on this. This type of ritual might be comforting, but at a different point in your grief. Admittedly, it may be something that you're never happy about. If you like the idea, you can make playlists of all the favorite songs you shared, a top-ten list of your favorite movies so that you can watch one each weekend, or a game night with the family.

Let your creativity direct you

You need not be an artist for creativity to help. Simply doodling, doing a paint-by-numbers, or jotting down your thoughts can provide catharsis.

You can, however, ritualize the creation of objects to honor your loved one and put all your emotions into the product. People who enjoy making things find it to be therapeutic, and the inspiration of your powerful emotions supplies an equally powerful creative drive.

Some of the most beautiful art in the world was created out of grief. You can find lists online of works that express grief. For example, Picasso, Munch, Van Gogh, and Goya often explored death in their works and painted expressions of their direct experiences with death. Composers work in requiems, authors write masterpieces, and actors channel their grief into amazing performances.

If you have a creative passion, you may find you cannot stop yourself from reaching out to it in your grief. This is natural. There is no shame in enjoying your passion while channeling your grief through it either. There really is no such thing as a "guilty" pleasure.

Remember, also, that creativity is not a "have-or-have-not" trait. If you decide that you'd like to take up a creative hobby or activity, do it, even if it's something you've never tried before.

And finally, a creative passion should never feel like work. If it gives you no pleasure, relief, or compensation, find something else.

WHEN YOU CAN STOP A RITUAL

Rituals are not rules. A ritual that causes you unnecessary pain or trouble will be of no help to you. We adopt rituals for a reason, but like all things, they can reach an end to their usefulness. But when you have attached a ritual to your loved one, the thought of "stopping" might seem disrespectful or alarming. If you stop a ritual, what does it mean?

We'll get to that. First, let's look at some reasons why it might be time to put a ritual to bed.

- It no longer comforts you. Consider this from several angles, however. If you dread a ritual, or simply have no enthusiasm for it, but know that afterward you will feel so much better for having done it, then you might want to keep going. If the ritual is of no benefit to you, but it's very beneficial to others and it's not directly harming you, you might also consider continuing for the sake of others. However, if you really don't care to do it, it provides no benefit to you or others, or it really causes you pain, you may relieve yourself of it.

- It has become prohibitive. Expenses, time, coordination—some rituals simply cannot be supported at the level you might want. It's not good to over-spend or exhaust yourself performing tasks.

- It's causing trouble. If a ritual is creating friction between you and someone else and damaging a re-lationship, this requires some reconsideration. You might want to have a conversation about this with the others involved and see if there is a solution.

Now, change is difficult, and our rituals are important. A ritual may be prohibitive, troublesome, and providing no comfort, but you still feel compelled and required to do it. I'm proba-bly not telling you anything you don't know already through your own common sense, but this is a hard time you are going through. I want to reassure you that there are options for rit-uals that have run their course.

- Change the frequency. If a daily ritual is becoming too much, change it to a weekly or monthly occur-rence, and see if that feels better.

- Adjust the ritual. Rituals are flexible. Try something else, a variation of the location, items involved, or time of day. If you were doing it alone, consider do-ing it with someone else now or vice versa. Rituals should not feel like work.

- Downsize (or upsize) the ritual. Most rituals can be adjusted to fit your mood, time, and budget. If a ritual has become overwhelming or underwhelm-ing, think about how to adjust its impact.

- Adopt a new ritual to replace the old one. Give your-self some time to consider what would feel more comforting and satisfying. Your emotions have a process, and what worked last year may no longer jibe with what you feel now. Creating a new ritual can be a wonderful way to reconnect, involving kids, friends, and family for their input. A new ritual can help you reevaluate why the ritual was meaningful to begin with.

- Tell others how you feel. If this is a family or group ritual, you may not think that it is OK to stop the ritual, and it may have never crossed your mind to tell others how much you don't like it. You are afraid of hurting feelings or looking bad in their eyes. But if they really are your family, tell them how you feel, and they might understand and work with you to make the ritual better or even excuse you from it.

Be kind to yourself. The desire to change or cease a ritual does not mean you love less or remember less than before. It means you have found a new way to love and remember.

♥

CHAPTER NINE
THE NEW RELATIONSHIP

In Chapter One, we discussed the stages of grief, including changes in how we *perceive* these stages as our personal and cultural understanding of grief continues to evolve. Modern grief models emphasize the importance of finding a connection to the deceased, allowing us to have a new relationship with them.

In the United States, we've gotten into a distressing habit of thinking or saying something along these lines: "Well, you simply must live without them now. They are gone forever! The more you try to connect, the more it will harm your ability to move on with your life." The implication of such statements is, "You may grieve for a while, but eventually you need to put it all aside and forge ahead in a life without your loved one." People who don't comply with this stricture are told that they "need to let go," and that "it's time to move on."

We are told to look for closure and acceptance. However, closure or acceptance in this death-denying culture implies we should shut our memories and feelings in a special box and set them aside. It's certainly OK to pull that box out sometimes and look through it, but its contents don't have a place in your new life.

So, for example, one might say, "On the anniversary of my mother's death each year, I visit her grave and speak to her." The weeks before and after this event might make one act differently, as some stages of grief may return. When Year Five or Year Six rolls around, someone might say, with the intention of helping, "Isn't it time for you to move on? You shouldn't do that to yourself."

But to someone grieving for the loss of a loved one, this is not only bad advice, it's a horrifying idea. If you are suffering loss right now, you may know this all too well: the idea of purposely cutting your loved one out of your life hurts almost as much as losing them in the first place.

Even if your culture convinces you that you should distance yourself and your feelings from the object of your loss, doing so is just a gateway to more misery. We are never so unhappy as when we try denying how we feel about something. We can only fool ourselves for so long.

The irony is that even if we try, we never "let go." It's not only painful but likely impossible. When a person is loved by you and is special and important to you, they are embedded in the fabric of your being. Their life impacts you, changes you, makes you more than you were before. This is exactly why losing them is so devastating. Thus, any attempt to sever that relationship asks you to sever a part of yourself.

Look around the world, and you'll see hundreds of cultures where the people revere, honor, and communicate with their deceased regularly. And these people are not "stuck in the past" or "wishing for things that can never happen" or "denying reality." They have done something far healthier and more joyful: they have found a new and gratifying relationship with those they have lost.

Does the new relationship replace the old one? Of course not. Forming a new relationship with the deceased isn't a cure for the grief of losing the old relationship. However, your loved one will remain an important part of your life and will be acknowledged as such.

Forming this new relationship is a matter of individual preference, and therefore it can come in infinite forms. We can adapt this relationship to what we need, what we believe, and what we feel our loved one would have wanted or what they now want. Yes, I believe that we can know what they want right now.

Each of us has different perceptions about what happens to the soul or spirit of a loved one. We may believe that they will return in a new form, that we will be reunited in the afterlife, or that their spirits can still speak to us through signs, dreams, and spiritual channels.

Even if you consider the entire concept of an afterlife or reincarnation to be completely imaginary, you can continue your relationship with a loved one. As I said, they have become part of the fabric of your being. As long as you live and remember, they are with you.

WHAT DOES A "NEW RELATIONSHIP" ACTUALLY MEAN?

If you have formed rituals that help you reach out, honor, and remember, you are already forming a new relationship. The rituals that feel best to you may prove to be the groundwork for the new relationship. The rituals incorporate your loved one into your life and make them part of your days. You keep their presence nearby.

There is no need to put a label on the relationship or to get the approval of anyone else that you're doing the right thing. In effect, the new relationship means whatever you want it to mean, provided that it is "meaning-full." Let me give you some examples.

- You can consider a loved one to now be your guardian angel, guiding force, or connection with the spiritual.

- They can be your inspiration for self-improvement. My friend Jane used her grief as the inspiration to try something new that she previously was afraid to try. She looked at a frightening challenge with new eyes, saying, "What was I so afraid of? Life is short, and I won't let this fear stop me any longer." She told me, "My grief made me brave." Now when Jane experiences success in her new field, she credits both herself and the loved one who inspired her.

- Your loved one can become the driving force for charity and generosity. My family and I support veterans' charities and charities that aim to bridge the tech gaps for children as a way to honor Michael's memory. It is quite common to see people rallying behind causes that their loved ones held dear or that promote cures or help for the conditions that might have caused the death of that loved one.

- You can finish a project or goal that they started or were thinking about starting. Were they writing a book, building a home, serving a cause, contributing to a project? What a wonderful way to honor their legacy.

- Your loved one can become the voice of your conscience in certain situations or problems. "What would they do in my place? What would they tell me?" You may imagine their answers based on how well you knew each other; you may also receive answers in the form of signs or dreams.

- Live in a way that you know will make them proud of you.

- Experience the things they loved or the things they didn't get a chance to do, and keep them in your thoughts while doing so.

- You can communicate with them as often as you like through the method of your choice: prayer, meditation, dreams, mediumship. You may write them letters or speak to their picture or grave site.

- You can tell others about them, including people who never met them in life. Tell of the things they did, the places they went, the things they said, their accomplishments, their dreams. Tell stories, write a book, use social media, make a movie—anything goes. Others can be invited to contribute to these stories as well.

- Your loved one can become the source of your wisdom and desire to help. This very book is just one of many ways I am still thinking about and working with Mike; I feel like he and I together want to provide comfort.

- Your loved one can be your connection to family and others. As we discussed, the bonds that we form when we grieve together are strong. We move into new levels of love and awareness when we share such experiences.

Those are just some of the ways in which you can keep a relationship with someone you have lost.

You may want to establish this relationship formally through the rituals we discussed in Chapter Eight. Or you may find that the relationship forms quite naturally without any intention on your part; if so, don't let others talk you out of it. Remember in our death-denying culture others may be anxious about relationships with the deceased because it reminds them that—oops —everyone dies.

WHEN THEY SAY THAT IT'S ALL IN YOUR HEAD

Our culture is determined to find "logical" explanations for anything and everything, especially when we're faced with someone else's grief. Yet when you lose a loved one, it is quite common to hear them, see them, or feel their presence nearby. "I heard my mother's voice," you might confess, only to be told some or all the following: "You imagined it," "You only *thought* you heard her," "That's your mind playing tricks on you," "That's just grief talking," and "It's all in your head."

If you see, hear, or feel your loved one close to you, you may embrace that experience to its fullest extent. Feeling such a connection can ease even the most awful pain of grief. Even if you do not believe it is possible for people to influence the world after death, even if you think it is an imaginary feeling, don't deny yourself the pleasure and relief of such a lucky moment.

Meanwhile, if others imply that your connection to a loved one is "all in your head," or somehow unhealthy, stunted, or troublesome, remember that they don't understand. They believe they are trying to help, but they're doing so in a way that helps them, alleviating their doubts and fears far more than it helps you. Don't let their doubts spoil what is a great comfort to you.

I want to let you know you're not crazy. So many people go through this.

Likewise, if someone tells you about experiencing a new connection with a loved one, don't feel obligated to disavow them of that belief because it strikes you as odd or unusual or you "don't believe in that kind of stuff." Listen, support them, and celebrate alongside them when the time is right. The only time you need to intervene is if someone truly seems to have trouble distinguishing between fantasy and reality to the point where they could hurt themselves or someone else, and that is a far cry from taking comfort in feeling close to a deceased loved one.

WHEN NEW AND OLD RELATIONSHIPS COLLIDE

I offer an example here of a painful situation that arose between the parents of a child who died. This is a true story relayed to me by a close friend who worked in an oncology social services department. In telling this story, I am not saying either party was right or wrong or that either made a mistake, but I am using it to illustrate how emotional turmoil can color the way we interpret the actions of others.

Ben and Dana had suffered a tragedy together. Their seven-year-old daughter, Charlotte, died from leukemia. It seemed that for years their entire lives had been about Charlotte's disease and trying to rescue her from it.

After Charlotte died, they were bereft on so many levels. They had lost their child—a devastating blow. They were left reeling in a "new normal" where there was no child, no cancer, no quest; so now, what could they do with themselves? And finally, they barely recognized each other. Their relationship, which might have been a source of support, just seemed to disintegrate under the stress, anger, and sadness. A major difficulty they met was that each was unwilling, unable, or perhaps just unready to see how the other was trying to relate to their daughter.

Thankfully, there were numerous support services in place, which Ben and Dana made use of.

One day their counselor got a very troubling series of calls. Dana was filing for divorce at once, based on something Ben had said and Dana's angry reaction to it. Pat, the counselor, could not get a definite answer about this "event" from either of them. Here is what she heard as she tried to parse out the source of this conflict.

Dana said, "Ben wants to act like Charlotte never existed."

Ben said, "Dana wants to act like Charlotte is still here with us."

It took some time for Pat to finally get to the bottom of the matter. Here's what had actually happened:

Ben suggested packing Charlotte's clothes and toys to donate to charity. Dana was horrified by the idea, not willing to give up anything belonging to their daughter. Their disagreement over that point had erupted into a terrible argument that resulted in those huge and unrealistic generalizations of each other's intentions.

Did packing up Charlotte's possessions really mean that Ben "wanted to act like Charlotte never existed?" Of course not. Ben had his own reasons for suggesting they give away Charlotte's things. He liked the idea of other children enjoying her toys and wearing her clothes. He felt that Charlotte, who was always generous with her possessions, would also like the idea, and together they could spread some happiness. It was *his* way of connecting to Charlotte.

Did refusing to pack up Charlotte's possessions really mean that Dana "wanted to pretend like Charlotte was still there?" Of course not. Dana considered Charlotte's possessions as a memorial where Dana could go and feel close to their daughter, and she needed these things to touch and see. It was *her* way of connecting to Charlotte.

We have no fly-on-the-wall viewpoint of exactly what was happening in that household, but it sounds as if communication had broken down between Charlotte's parents. They certainly needed the help of a neutral party, time to adjust to each other's viewpoints, a path toward compromise, and a lot of patience and understanding. Calling their counselor, Pat, was a good start.

Your "relationships" with those who have died are complicated. Others may not fully understand the reasons because what they feel and need is quite different. Communicate your feelings, but also listen to what others have to say. No two people will feel quite the same way. The best-case scenario is to do what feels right for yourself without intentionally disrupting what feels right for others. If your "new relationship" really becomes a point of contention, however, the guidelines still apply: talk it out, seek a neutral opinion, find a compromise, and give yourself and others time to adjust.

LETTING GO, CLOSURE, MOVING ON, AND ACCEPTANCE … IN CONTEXT

Grief is an unpredictable ride. As we have discussed, it is important that we ride it all the way; there are no shortcuts. Depending on our personalities, our circumstances, and our available support, it is possible to get "stuck" along the way.

There does come a point when you must "let go" of something, but it's not your loved one. You can experience "closure," but it doesn't have to mean an ending. "Moving on" might seem like a betrayal, but what you really mean is that you are "moving forward." And you can "accept" that things are different now without needing to ignore or deny someone's importance. These are just words and terms. Context is everything.

Here is an example: If you keep a memorial to your loved one and you cry there once a week and someone tells you to "you really need to let go," they are probably reacting to their own discomfort. But if you have been in bed for two months and haven't the energy to shower or feed yourself, and someone says, "You really need to let go," they are more likely referring to the guilt, anger, or depression that is keeping you pinned down in this lonely place and impacting your health.

Your first response to their suggestion may be anger because it feels like they are telling you to forget about the one you have lost. That's really not the case, however. I hope you can understand when I say that there is beauty and value in grief, but these things must be found along a difficult road. There is no shame in seeking help if you are overwhelmed along that journey and cannot seem to move forward.

Beauty and value? It may be hard to believe that. You might doubt that those feelings could ever come from grief.

If you have suffered grief before, you may look back on that experience and know that such feelings did eventually happen. If you have never been through something like this before, put some faith in your own resilience and love. Loss will always hurt, but love is more powerful, and you will always have that too. Your "new relationship" acknowledges love in all its power.

CONCLUSION - THE UNEXPECTED GIFTS OF GRIEF

The term "harnessing grief" is one that I got from Maryann, the trusted advisor and the medium who helps me speak to my husband. What does it mean? Like everything else, when it comes to the experience of grief, the meaning will change a bit from person to person.

I have learned—and I'm still learning—that we never "get over" grief, but we can change how we carry it. To me, harnessing my grief means moving from unspeakable loss and despair to using that grief as a force of good, helping not only myself but others.

Sometimes it's hard to talk about grief as a "good thing" or a "positive thing" because it just hurts so much. The idea of "finding a silver lining" in this storm seems impossible or maybe even offensive.

We grievers (and that's all of us, sooner or later) must look at our situations from a real perspective. There has been a painful change in our lives. It's unfair and unbelievable, and because this is life, it's unavoidable. There's nothing we can do to "undo" what happened. What we choose to do afterward, however, makes a huge difference. Choosing to harness our grief toward a positive outcome rather than a negative one is how we can respect ourselves and the people for whom we grieve.

In this final chapter, therefore, I will talk about the unexpected gifts that can come with grief. Here are some I have experienced myself and some that others have found. You may find some of your own. These bittersweet gifts are there for you to use, even though you may honestly and understandably want to reject them, send them back, lashing out against whatever cruel hand is offering them. You know what? That's OK too. The unexpected gifts of grief will wait until you are ready.

THE GIFTS

You recognize that grief has changed you, but it has not destroyed your fundamental self. Whatever course your grief takes, it will rewire your thinking. That's all right; all important experiences do that. For a long time during your grief, you might have felt adrift, lost, like a stranger in your own life. You are, nevertheless, still you, still capable of love, joy, remembrance, and laughter.

You are kinder, wiser, and more empathetic toward others. Suffering can bring out the best and the worst in us. Sometimes the "worst" will still try to have its day. But on other days, the "best" is going to win. Having suffered and survived, you can reach out to others who need help and reassurance. We can never truly know each other's pain, but having suffered our own, we certainly recognize the landmarks.

You are braver. For a while it seemed like a breeze could shatter you; you felt so broken and lost. But as your grief moved forward, so did your strength. What, exactly, can life throw at you that you can't handle? You've been forged in fire. And as for people who get upset about the "little things," well, you're no longer one of them.

Your personality's more dramatic aspects have "evened out." Grief has a way of smoothing rough edges, maturing you, making you self-aware, making you refine yourself. So perhaps, prior to your grief experience, you had some personality extremes that could be problematic. Hey, nobody's perfect. Once you process grief, you may find that you're just better about certain things than you used to be. Maybe you're less egocentric, more generous, less critical, or more focused. There is no need to rush this or push yourself to become something you're not, however. Grief can also make our personalities unmanageable at times. Did I mention that nobody's perfect?

Your creativity increases, along with your motivation to create. A desire to create often seems proportionate to pain; people who have been through these trials turn to creativity. You may blossom in this exquisite combination of joy and pain to make beautiful, influential things to inspire, aid, enjoy, share, and keep memories alive. In Chapter Eight (on rituals), we talked about how grief inspires great art. You can find comfort in those works, knowing the artist has been through an experience like yours; likewise, your creative insights might do the same for someone else.

You accept what cannot be changed. No longer do you waste your time or energy fuming and fretting over things that are outside of your control. You understand the boundaries of your control and excel within them.

You have an increased appreciation for life, beauty, and time. This is a priceless skill. How many times have you heard that we must all "stop and smell the roses?" Now you cherish the daily pleasures of life and make the most of your time.

You treasure memories and strive to make new ones. Nothing will teach you the value of memory so much as grief. And "making memories," you will learn, is not about taking photographs of events or spending money on vacations or creating the "perfect" moment. Memories are made when we stop, recognize where we are and what we have, and appreciate it fully. You have learned to do this daily.

You are in tune with something beyond yourself. A connection with the afterlife, the spiritual, the beyond is a great consolation at any point in your life. You no longer fear "what comes next" because you know it will be all right.

Do you recognize any of these gifts? If not, they may come later, tomorrow, next year. When an unexpected gift of grief comes to you, it may break your heart a little bit even as you give thanks. It might make you laugh or cry again or raise a toast or say a prayer. Think of how your loved one would react, what they might say, how proud he or she is of you.

NEVER THE LAST WORDS

On the last day I had with Mike, I was a mess. I suffered a strong reaction to a flu vaccine, so I was, for all purposes sick with the flu and definitely not at my best. Being sick was hard enough, plus I had small children who needed looking after, and so many things to consider with our new business. I was honestly overwhelmed and miserable.

Mike came into the house with a "care package" of supplies. He just wanted me to feel better. I remember him bringing cold medicine, water and Gatorade, plus junk food and lottery scratch-offs for fun. That man always knew how to cheer me up. Then, he did something so oddball and wonderful and romantic.

He knelt next to me on the side of the couch—where I huddled in my old PJs, without makeup, with swollen nose and puffy eyes and tissues scattered everywhere, and he said, "Sweetheart, I may not say this enough, but I need you to know how proud I am of you and how much I love you." I had to laugh with my wonderful, patient husband.

It was perfect: a perfect thing to say, a perfect moment. I'll treasure that forever. Though it might have been our "last" day the way we were then, I do not believe it was the end. There was, and is, still more to come.

So, my friends in grief, this is how we conclude this book, without a real conclusion, because nothing is ever *really* over when love is involved. Love doesn't recognize time or distance. Love is forever. Love is the foundation of grief, but it is also the balm to grief, the outcome of grief, and the conqueror of the darker corners of grieving.

I believe that Mike and I created this book together in hopes that our experience would help anyone else who suffered loss and the long, sometimes difficult, sometimes fascinating, sometimes awful, sometimes beautiful road that follows.

I'm no expert in psychology or medicine, spirituality, or religion. But I'm an expert on grief—my own—because no one else can be, as you are an expert in yours. I'm not done either, not with grieving and not with growing. Things will be different from what we thought they would be, but we're going to be all right.

I want you to care for yourself, be kind to yourself, and allow yourself to find happiness again. I will do the same.

– Alexandra

♥

ACKNOWLEDGMENTS

My thanks to ...

... Jenna Gelow Designs, for her cover art and amazing graphic design work.

... Maryann Kelly, for being a trusted advisor and compassionately protecting and sharing my connection with Michael.

... My family—Mom, Dad, Shannon, Dan, Hendrix, Lucas, and Ava—for always inspiring me to do good in Michael's name, and

... Michael, for everything. I was blessed to meet my soulmate. I hope our experiences can help others on the journey of grief.

ABOUT ATMOSPHERE PRESS

Atmosphere Press is an independent, full-service publisher for excellent books in all genres and for all audiences. Learn more about what we do at atmospherepress.com.

We encourage you to check out some of Atmosphere's latest releases, which are available at Amazon.com and via order from your local bookstore:

Finding Us, by Kristin Rehkamp

The Ideological and Political System of Banselism, by Royard Halmonet Vantion (Ancheng Wang)

Unconditional: Loving and Losing an Addict, by Lizzy and Adam

Telling Tales and Sharing Secrets, by Jackie Collins, Diana Kinared, and Sally Showalter

Nursing Homes: A Missionary's Journey Through Heaven's Waiting Room, by Tim Eatman Ph.D.

Timeline of Stars, by Joe Adcock

A Boy Who Loved Me, by Wilson Semitti

The Injustice in Justice, by Charmaine Loverin

Living in the Gray, by Katie Weber

Living with Veracity, Dying with Dignity, by Alison Clay-Duboff

Noah's Rejects, by Rob Kagan

A lot of Questions (with no answers)?, by Jordan Neben

Cowboy from Prague: An Immigrant's Pursuit of the American Dream, by Charles Ota Heller

Sleeping Under the Bridge, by Melissa Baker

The Only Prayer I Ever Have to Say Is Thank You, by M. Kaya Hill

Amygdala Blue, by Paul Lomax

A Caregiver's Love Story, by Nancie Wiseman Attwater

♥

ABOUT THE AUTHOR

Alexandra founded McGroarty & Co. Consulting and serves as the lead Human Resources consultant. Alex is a certified Diversity Professional as well as a Certified Professional Coach. She recently obtained a graduate certificate from Cornell University in sustainability.

Alexandra lives with her two children, Lucas and Ava, their two dogs, Sugar and Fiona, and a feisty cat named Scrambles, in New Jersey. In her free time, she likes to spend time with family, travel, and volunteer in the Greater Philadelphia area.

Made in United States
Orlando, FL
17 December 2023

41154418R00071